RON RHODES

40 DAYS
THROUGH BIBLE
PROPHECY

HARVEST PROPHECY
An Imprint of Harvest House Publishers

Scripture versions used in this book are listed at the back of the book

Cover design by Studio Gearbox, Chris Gilbert

Cover Photo © Jason Busa, Netfalls Remy Musser, Chubykin Arkady, Vadim Sadovski, Z-River / Shutterstock

Interior design by Rockwell Davis

For bulk, special sales, or ministry purchases, please call 1-800-547-8979. Email: Customerservice@hhpbooks.com

This logo is a federally registered trademark of the Hawkins Children's LLC. Harvest House Publishers, Inc., is the exclusive licensee of this trademark.

40 Days Through Bible Prophecy
Copyright © 2023 by Ron Rhodes
Published by Harvest House Publishers
Eugene, Oregon 97408
www.harvesthousepublishers.com

ISBN 978-0-7369-8653-3 (pbk)
ISBN 978-0-7369-8654-0 (eBook)

Library of Congress Control Number: 2022938744

Printed in the United States of America

22 23 24 25 26 27 28 29 30 / BP / 10 9 8 7 6 5 4 3 2 1

To Kerri, David, and Kylie—
May God's love, joy, and peace be your daily experience!
(Galatians 5:22)

Acknowledgments

My heart is brimming with thanks to God for the wondrous gift of my family—Kerri, David, and Kylie. They are my support team, my prayer team, and my daily source of inspiration! "I thank my God through Jesus Christ for all of you" (Romans 1:8).

I am deeply grateful for my extended time with the late Dr. John F. Walvoord, my primary prophecy mentor at Dallas Theological Seminary (DTS) back in the 1980s. I continue to appreciate the late Dr. J. Dwight Pentecost at DTS for his comprehensive courses on the prophetic books of Daniel and Revelation, as well as his course on the life of Christ. I will never forget those classes. I am also indebted to the late Drs. Charles Ryrie and Norman Geisler for instilling in me a strong understanding of the inspiration, reliability, and authority of Scripture—including *prophetic* Scripture. The insightful teachings of Walvoord, Pentecost, Ryrie, and Geisler played a significant role in shaping my views on biblical prophecy.

Continued heartfelt appreciation goes to the entire staff at Harvest House Publishers—especially Bob Hawkins and Steve Miller. It has been a pleasure working with this fine publisher through these many years! The professionalism and commitment to truth among the staff are shining examples among Christian publishers. "God...will not forget how hard you have worked for him" (Hebrews 6:10 NLT).

Most important of all, I remain ever grateful to the Lord Jesus for the opportunity He has given me to serve Him during this short earthly life. "Every day I will bless you and praise your name forever and ever" (Psalm 145:2).

Come soon, Lord!

Contents

40 Days
Through Bible Prophecy

People sometimes ask me why I write so many prophecy books. My answer lies in the following statistics:

- Out of the 23,210 verses in the Old Testament, 6,641 of them are prophetic. *That's 28.5 percent.*
- Out of the 7,914 verses in the New Testament, 1,711 of them are prophetic. *That's 21.5 percent.*
- Merging the Old and New Testaments, some 8,352 of the Bible's 31,124 verses are prophetic. That means **27 percent of the Bible is prophetic.**

Twenty-seven percent! That's a considerable portion of the Bible! It indicates to me that Bible prophecy is important to God. For that reason, it is important to me. And that's why I write prophecy books.

Bible prophecy is especially relevant because of what is transpiring today. If these are the "last days," as I believe they are, then we would expect to see certain developments in the world—developments that relate specifically to the end times as prophesied in Scripture. These developments include a falling away from the truth, the widespread embracing of doctrinal error, a significant moral decline, a growing tolerance for all things evil, and a widespread outbreak of sexual sins and perversions.

We would further expect to see a steady diminishing of religious freedom, the global persecution of God's people, Israel being a sore spot in the world, ever-escalating conflict in the Middle East, efforts being made toward the rebuilding of the Jewish temple, and the stage being set for a massive Russian/Muslim invasion of Israel. Also expected are the steady rise of globalism, political and economic strides toward establishing a revived Roman Empire, and the emergence of a cashless world in preparation for the antichrist's control of the world economy during the tribulation period.

It is sobering to ponder how all of these, in varying degrees, are trending in our present day—sure indicators that we are living in the end times. They are foreshadowing the events that will transpire during the coming tribulation period.[1] I will address these matters throughout this book.

A 40-DAY APPROACH

The unique feature of this book is that it divides all the various topics related to Bible prophecy into 40 short chapters. The book can easily be completed in 40 days. This means that in just 40 days...

- You will have a good handle on all the major prophetic events that will occur in the future.

- You will become familiar with all the prominent personalities of the end times.

- You will have a good grasp of the proper chronology of prophetic events.

- You will become well familiar with unique terms associated with prophecy—terms like "the rapture," "the millennial kingdom," and "the eternal state."

I will be your tour guide for this journey through prophetic Scripture. I will help you understand what you need to know, while avoiding unnecessary clutter. In addition to concise descriptions and Bible exposition of crucial verses, each day's reading will feature "Fast Facts" on important topics, "Frequently Asked Questions," "Today's Big Ideas," and "Today's Transforming Truths." You will find this approach highly informative, easy to grasp, fast moving, and inspiring.

Definitions of essential prophetic terms, **key historical insights**, and **important points** will be highlighted in shadowed boxes.

Once the 40 days are completed, you will not only have a grasp of the main components of Bible prophecy, you will also have a good grasp on other issues that are relevant to your spiritual life. You will come to understand that:

- God truly knows the future.
- The Bible—which is brimming with God's prophecies of the future—is the Word of God and can be trusted.
- God is in sovereign control of all that occurs in the world.
- God is now providentially guiding human history toward its prophetic culmination.
- God has a plan for humanity—*and He has a plan for you individually.*
- God will one day providentially cause good to triumph over evil.
- There is a new world coming—*the best is yet to come.*
- We will all get body upgrades—*resurrected or glorified bodies that never age, get sick, or die.*
- We will experience a joyful reunion with all our Christian loved ones in heaven.
- The Lord is coming sooner than we think!

You will find that daily exposure of your mind to these glorious scriptural truths over 40 days will help build an eternal perspective in you that will fortify your spiritual life for years to come. *I guarantee it!*

If you are already well acquainted with the study of Bible prophecy, this book will also benefit you. It is good to infuse our minds daily with God's Word—including God's prophetic Word. Regular exposure—even *repetitive* exposure—to God's Word brings great blessing. Joshua

1:8 tells us: "This Book of the Law shall not depart from your mouth, but you shall meditate on it day and night, so that you may be careful to do according to all that is written in it. For then you will make your way prosperous, and then you will have good success." Proverbs 3:1 instructs: "My son, do not forget my teaching." The psalmist muses: "I will meditate on your precepts and fix my eyes on your ways. I will delight in your statutes; I will not forget your word" (Psalm 119:15-16). Repetitive exposure to God's truths virtually lives in such passages. So do not hesitate to review God's prophetic Word regularly.

OUR WONDROUS, ALL-KNOWING GOD

In many of my prophecy books, I have emphasized right up front that Bible prophecy finds its origin in God, who alone knows the future. I do this intentionally because people can get so enthralled about knowing the future that they unintentionally fail to fully appreciate God's greatness in relation to prophecy. Here is something to remember: *The greater your understanding of God's greatness, the stronger your conviction will be about the prophecies that emanate from Him!*

I could write a book about God's greatness (and maybe I will one day). However, for now, here is what I want you to know: Because God transcends time—*because He is above time*—He can see the past, present, and future as a single intuitive act. God's knowledge of all things is from the vantage point of eternity so that all events in the past, present, and future are encompassed in one ever-present "now" to Him. I know that boggles the mind. *The main thing to grasp is that God truly knows the future.*

Scripture reveals God knows all things, both actual and possible (Matthew 11:21-24). He knows all things past (Isaiah 41:22), present (Hebrews 4:13), and future (Isaiah 46:10). Because He knows all things, there can be no increase or decrease in His knowledge. Psalm 147:5 affirms that God's understanding "is beyond measure." His knowledge is infinite (Psalm 33:13-15; 139:11-12; 147:5; Proverbs 15:3; Isaiah 40:14; 46:10; Acts 15:18; 1 John 3:20; Hebrews 4:13). Look up these verses—*they will inspire you and bless you!*

Because God's knowledge is infinite, you and I can trust Bible prophecy. God wants us to *know for sure* that we can trust Bible prophecy. He does not want there to be any doubt in our minds. He assures us: "I am God, and there is no other; I am God, and there is none like me, declaring the end from the beginning and from ancient times things not yet done, saying, 'My counsel shall stand, and I will accomplish all my purpose'...I have spoken, and I will bring it to pass; I have purposed, and I will do it" (Isaiah 46:9-11).

When I first became a Christian, the thing that convinced me of God's awesomeness and the trustworthiness of Bible prophecy is that there are over 100 messianic prophecies in the Old Testament that predict specific details relating to the first coming of Jesus. *All of them* were literally fulfilled, to the crossing of the "t" and the dotting of the "i." For example, the Old Testament prophesied the Messiah would be from the seed of a woman (Genesis 3:15); the offspring of Abraham (Genesis 12:3); from the tribe of Judah (Genesis 49:10); the son of David (Jeremiah 23:5-6); conceived of a virgin (Isaiah 7:14); born in Bethlehem (Micah 5:2); the heralded Messiah (Isaiah 40:3); the coming King (Zechariah 9:9); the sacrificial lamb who would be crucified for our sins (Isaiah 53); the one who would be pierced in His side (Zechariah 12:10); the one who would die around AD 33 (Daniel 9:24-25); and the one who would rise from the dead (Psalm 2, 16). These—and a multitude of others—were literally fulfilled in Jesus' first coming.

Since this is true, you can also trust what prophetic Scripture reveals about Christ's second coming and all the prophetic events that lead up to it. Never doubt it! Drive the stake into the ground today. Affirm with me:

I know I can trust Bible prophecies regarding the future because God has been 100 percent accurate in all His prophecies in the past. He has set a trustworthy precedent. I will never doubt Him. I will believe whatever He says. It simply remains for me to learn what the Bible teaches about prophecy. Once learned, it will immediately become a firm conviction in my mind. The matter is settled! There is no hesitation. I will trust what I learn about prophecy from the Bible because I believe in a trustworthy God!

MY PRAYER FOR YOU

As is true with all my writings, I pray that this book will inform your mind and touch your heart. Christian theology that does not touch the heart—*that fails to resonate with your inner spirit so that it changes you*—has failed at its task. That is one reason I am excited about this book.

My prayer is that this book will cause a paradigm shift in how you view this present world. The more your present life is informed by the glorious truths of the prophetic future, the more you will gain an eternal perspective that will help you navigate the difficult circumstances you might face during this short earthly life.

So, my friend, let's dive into the Scriptures together. Let's be open-minded about what God wants to teach us. And let us resolve to allow God to do His life-changing work in us as His Word saturates our hearts and minds.

Pray along with me:

> *Lord, I ask You to open my eyes and enhance my understanding so that I can grasp what You want me to learn in the next 40 days. I also ask You to enable me, by Your Spirit, to apply the truths I learn in my daily life and be guided moment by moment by Your Word. Thank You in Jesus' name. Amen.*

Day 1

Prophets and Prophecy:
What You Need to Know

Two definitions set the context for today's lesson:

- **Prophecy** involves God's specific revelations about future events and personalities. In modern vernacular, some describe prophecy as "history written in advance." God communicates His prophetic revelations through human prophets.
- The word ***prophet*** comes from the Hebrew word *nabi*. It carries the idea of "God's spokesman." In the Bible, we find both *major prophets* (the "big wheels") and *minor prophets* (the "small fries").

The major prophets are Isaiah, Jeremiah, Ezekiel, and Daniel. These guys seem larger than life. The minor prophets—lesser-known but still significant—are Hosea, Joel, Amos, Obadiah, Jonah, Micah, Nahum, Habakkuk, Zephaniah, Haggai, Zechariah, and Malachi. Here's a crucial point:

The prophetic words spoken by the minor prophets are just as much from God as the prophetic words spoken by the major prophets. All messages from God are important.

A comparison of the Old and New Testaments confirms how God spoke through human prophets. In the Old Testament, God's human prophet spoke forth a prophetic word. Later, in the pages of the New Testament, we discover that God Himself spoke through that prophet. The prophet was literally a *mouthpiece for God.*

To illustrate, the psalmist made a proclamation that begins in Psalm 95:7. Hebrews 3:7 later informs us that the Holy Spirit was speaking through the psalmist in that passage. Likewise, the psalmist made a statement beginning in Psalm 45:6. And Hebrews 1:8 later tells us that God was speaking through the psalmist in that statement.

What about the major and minor prophets? We see the same thing. The major prophet Isaiah made a proclamation in Isaiah 7:14. Matthew 1:22-23 later informs us that the Lord was speaking through Isaiah in that verse. The minor prophet Hosea made a statement in Hosea 11:1. Then Matthew 2:15 later tells us that the Lord was speaking through Hosea in that verse.

I encourage you to look up these verses. In each case, God (or the Lord, or the Holy Spirit) spoke through a prophet acting as a *human mouthpiece* for God.

This convinces me we can trust Bible prophecy. Prophecy comes from God, and everything God says through a prophet will happen (2 Peter 1:21; Isaiah 48:3; 42:8-9). God has never been wrong! He has a 100 percent accuracy rate.

Of course, some phony prophets and psychics have *claimed* to be accurate. In every case, however, these false prophets and psychics have set forth "prophecies" that are incredibly vague. A psychic, for example, might inform a client: "I foresee a romance in your future." Or perhaps: "Good fortune will come your way in the next few decades." Or perhaps: "I foresee an illness in the coming years for one of your elderly parents." It is easy to find "fulfillments" for such generalized "prophecies."

This is entirely unlike biblical prophecies. As Mark Hitchcock put it, "The biblical prophets did not peddle predictions that were so vague and general they could be adjusted to any situation. The prophecies recorded in the Bible are very precise and so specific that when they are fulfilled, it's very clear there's something unique and special about them."[2]

I could share many biblical prophecies to prove this point—and before you come to the end of this book, you will become acquainted with a large number of biblical prophecies that prove this point. For now, I will give you three: The Old Testament prophesies that (1) Jesus would be born *in Bethlehem* (Micah 5:2), (2) *by a virgin* (Isaiah 7:14), (3) and that He would be *crucified* (Isaiah 53:12; Zechariah 12:10). There are more than a hundred other precise prophecies in the Old Testament that were fulfilled in the person of Jesus. Notice there is nothing vague about these prophecies!

FAST FACTS ON PROPHETS

God directly chose His prophets (Jeremiah 1:5; Luke 1:13-16). And they came from all walks of life—from farmers (Amos 7:14) to princes (Genesis 23:6).

God's prophets had two primary roles: (1) On some occasions, they directed their words at specific contemporary situations or problems that needed attention right at the time when they were speaking. (2) On other occasions, they foretold the future based on divine revelation.

The prophets typically prefaced their words with "Thus saith the Lord." Their words were not their own but came from God. Tim LaHaye and Ed Hindson tell us: "Their messages were supernatural, not natural. They were derived neither from observation nor intellectual thought, but from knowing God and speaking with Him."[3] The divine source of their words gave their words authority.

These prophets were always 100 percent accurate. If a prophet was not perfectly accurate, the people were to stone him to death as a false prophet (Deuteronomy 13:1-5; 18:20-22).

Because Christ literally fulfilled more than 100 Old Testament prophecies in His first coming, we have strong confidence that the far more numerous prophecies of the second coming will find just as literal fulfillments.

FREQUENTLY ASKED QUESTIONS

Are there any prophets today?

Some Christians claim there are prophets in the church today. Scripture reveals, however, that the church "was built on the foundation of the apostles and prophets" (Ephesians 2:20). Once a foundation is built, it never needs to be built *again*. Once the foundation of a building is laid, a structure is built *upon it*. In like fashion, the "building" of the church rests on the foundation of the apostles and prophets that lived back in Bible times. We do not need to build any new foundations with new apostles and new prophets.

Some may claim to have a "gift of prophecy" in the loose sense of *forth-telling* (or speaking forth) teachings found in the Bible. But there are certainly no "foretelling" prophets on the level of Isaiah, Ezekiel, and Daniel today.

Will there be any prophets in the future?

Though there are not true prophets in the church today on the level of Isaiah, Ezekiel, and Daniel, that will change during the future seven-year tribulation period. During that time, God will raise up two mighty prophetic witnesses who have the same miraculous powers as Moses and Elijah (Revelation 11:1-15). Some Bible expositors believe the two witnesses may *actually be* Moses and Elijah. Three primary reasons are offered:

1. Moses and Elijah are the two most influential figures in Jewish history. It would therefore make good sense that they are on the scene during the tribulation period, during which God deals heavily with the Jews.

2. Both appeared on the Mount of Transfiguration with Jesus (Matthew 17:3), thus showing their importance and centrality in God's unfolding purposes.

3. Both the Old Testament and Jewish tradition expected Moses (Deuteronomy 18:15, 18) and Elijah (Malachi 4:5) to return in the end times.

Of course, we cannot be dogmatic on this. God may raise up two entirely new prophets during this time.

Do prophets ever make mistakes?

Some people claim the prophet Jonah made a mistake when he prophesied God would overthrow Nineveh in 40 days. Jonah's prediction did not come to pass.

Jonah, however, did not make a mistake because he told the Ninevites precisely what God told him to say (Jonah 3:1-2). There was an apparent "repentance clause" built into Jonah's prophecy. The Ninevites understood that God would overthrow Nineveh in 40 days *unless they repented* (verses 5-9). Based on how the Ninevites responded in repentance to Jonah's prophecy, God withdrew the threatened punishment.

Jeremiah 18:7-8 provides an important backdrop. In this passage, God affirmed: "If at any time I declare concerning a nation or a kingdom, that I will pluck up and break down and destroy it, and if that nation, concerning which I have spoken, turns from its evil, I will relent of the disaster that I intended to do to it." This is the "repentance clause" I was talking about.

Nineveh renounced its evil, and God responded with mercy (see Exodus 32:14; 2 Samuel 24:16; Amos 7:3, 6). God always loves to show mercy where repentance is evident.

TODAY'S BIG IDEAS

- Prophets are God's mouthpieces. God reveals the future through them.

- Prophecies delivered through these prophets are 100 percent accurate.

- Because all the prophecies relating to the first coming of Christ were fulfilled literally, we may expect that all the prophecies of the second coming (and the events leading up to the second coming) will be fulfilled just as literally.

TODAY'S TRANSFORMING TRUTHS

- The Bible is God's revelation to us, God speaking to us, and God instructing us (Psalm 119; 2 Timothy 3:15-17). About 25 percent of what God reveals in the Bible is prophetic. You can trust every word, sentence, and paragraph of the prophecies found in the Bible.

- God's prophetic plan encompasses not only the world *but also each one of us*. We need to firmly anchor in our minds that God has His eyes on us and has a wonderful plan for our future (Jeremiah 29:11; Psalm 32:8; Proverbs 3:5-6; Romans 8:28). It is good to begin each day with this recognition.

Day 2

Why Prophecy Is a Big Deal

I think Bible prophecy is a big deal. I say this because prophecy brings tremendous blessing to believers. The book of Revelation offers this wonderful promise: "Blessed is the one who reads aloud the words of this prophecy, and blessed are those who hear, and who keep what is written in it, for the time is near" (Revelation 1:3). During New Testament times, a person would read from Scripture while everyone else listened carefully. The reader and listeners all got blessed. There are six other pronouncements of special blessing in the book of Revelation (14:13; 16:15; 19:9; 20:6; 22:7, 14). *I want that blessing! Don't you?*

Another reason Bible prophecy is a big deal is that it strengthens our convictions about crucial Christian beliefs. For example, prophecy reinforces our conviction that the God of the Bible is the one true God. After all, false gods cannot predict the future like the true God can. In the Old Testament, God issued this challenge to the false gods and idols: "Tell us what is to happen...declare to us the things to come. Tell us what is to come hereafter, that we may know that you are gods" (Isaiah 41:22-23). The false gods obviously could not comply since they didn't even exist. God then affirmed in no uncertain terms: "I am God, and there is no other; I am God, and there is none like me, declaring the end from the beginning and from ancient times things not yet done, saying, 'My counsel shall stand, and I will accomplish all my purpose'" (46:9-10).

Bible prophecy also strengthens our conviction that the Bible is the Word of God. After all, only God knows the prophetic future—and He has recorded His prophecies *in the Bible alone*, not in any other so-called "holy book." The more than 100 Old Testament prophecies that were

fulfilled with 100 percent accuracy in the first coming of Christ constitute decisive proof that the Bible is the Word of God and can be trusted.

Bible prophecy can also be an excellent tool for evangelism. Peter
preached a powerful sermon on the day of Pentecost (Acts 2). Supernatural phenomena occurred that day, and Peter informed the enormous crowd that all of it had been prophesied in the Old Testament
(verse 16). Once Peter spoke about prophecy to the crowd, he informed
the people that salvation is available by calling upon the name of the
Lord (verse 21). *Some 3,000 people became believers that day!* Peter used
prophecy as an evangelistic tool—and you and I can do the same.

Back in the 1970s, my family regularly attended a liberal church.

> **Liberal churches** typically teach that the Bible is man-made,
> the miracles in the Bible didn't occur, Jesus is not truly God,
> and Jesus is not the only way of salvation.

I had no idea I was attending a false church. I was biblically illiter-
ate. I then started reading some books on Bible prophecy, and these
caused a major paradigm shift in my life. As a direct result of prophecy,
I became a Christian, left the liberal church, joined a good biblically
based church, eventually attended Dallas Theological Seminary and
obtained both a Master's of Theology degree and a Doctorate of Theology degree, and have been serving the Lord ever since.

I am a living testimony to how prophecy can be used in evangelism.
Bible prophecy entirely changed the course of my life.

There is yet another reason that Bible prophecy is a big deal. Anything Jesus talked about is a big deal—and Jesus spoke at length about
prophecy in His Olivet Discourse.

> **The Olivet Discourse** is so named because Jesus was sitting
> on the Mount of Olives when He delivered it (Matthew
> 24:3).

The disciples asked Jesus, "Tell us, when will these things be, and what will be the sign of your coming and of the end of the age?" (verse 3). The Olivet Discourse is His response to this question. Jesus predicted the appearance of false christs, wars, earthquakes, famines, the profaning of the Jewish temple, cosmic disturbances (Matthew 24:4-28), the sign of His coming (verses 29-31), and how the end times will be much like the days of Noah (verses 36-39).

A final reason Bible prophecy is a big deal is that many ancient prophecies seem to be coming to pass in our day. (The rebirth of Israel in 1948 is a great example.) Prophecy expert Mark Hitchcock tells us that "35 percent of Americans are paying more attention now to how the news might relate to the end of the world. Seventeen percent believe that the end of the world will happen in their lifetime, and 59 percent believe that the prophecies of the Book of Revelation will come true."[4] Every passing year that world conditions continue to worsen, the bigger deal prophecy becomes.

FAST FACTS ON HOW PROPHECY HELPS US WHEN LIFE THROWS A PUNCH

Bible prophecy strengthens our faith when we face hard times. The original recipients of the book of Revelation were suffering from severe persecution. Some were even being martyred (Revelation 2:13). The book of Revelation was intended to give these suffering saints a sense of hope that would help them patiently endure their pain. The underlying lesson of the book of Revelation is that human suffering is temporal, but our eternal life with God lasts forever.

Bible prophecy comforts us when a Christian loved one dies. First Thessalonians 4:13-17 reveals that all Christians will have a grand reunion in heaven. We will all be together again. Because of this, the apostle Paul tells us to "encourage one another with these words" (verse 18). As J.C. Ryle put it, "Our pleasant communion with our kind Christian friends is only broken off for a small moment and is soon to be eternally resumed. These eyes of ours shall once more look upon their faces, and these ears of ours shall once more hear them speak...Blessed and happy indeed will that meeting be—better a thousand times than the parting!"[5]

Bible prophecy assures us that God will triumph over all evil. In the afterlife, the antichrist, the false prophet, Satan, demons, and humans who have rejected Christ will be put in eternal quarantine in the lake of fire (Revelation 19:20; 20:10-15). Meanwhile, resurrected and glorified believers—no longer having a sin nature—will live directly in God's presence in the New Jerusalem, the eternal city of the redeemed (21:2-5). *Evil will be gone forever!*

FREQUENTLY ASKED QUESTIONS

Doesn't prophecy involve a great deal of sensationalism?

While some people have unfortunately fallen prey to sensationalism, Scripture urges against it. First Peter 4:7 instructs us: "The end of all things is at hand; therefore be self-controlled and sober-minded." The Holman Christian Standard version translates the latter part of the verse "be serious and disciplined" (HCSB). The New King James Version puts it, "be serious and watchful" (NKJV). The Amplified Bible renders it, "keep sound minded and self-restrained" (AMPCE). Such words leave no room for sensationalism.

Doesn't prophecy involve a lot of speculation?

Some Christians have indeed promoted speculative ideas about Bible prophecy. But that should not dampen our enthusiasm for a legitimate study of the end times. As noted previously, more than 25 percent of the Bible is prophetic. It is unwise to ignore a fourth of the Bible simply because a few unbalanced interpreters are out there. Let us commit to regularly studying Bible prophecy, and do so in a thoughtful and balanced way. This book will help you do that. Stay the course!

Don't many Christians engage in "newspaper exegesis" when studying prophecy?

Some Christian interpreters have indeed fallen prey to so-called "newspaper exegesis."

Newspaper exegesis involves taking a newspaper's headlines and then forcing them into the interpretation of biblical prophecies.

I do not use newspaper exegesis, nor do the books listed in this book's bibliography. Such forced exegesis is unworthy of serious Bible students. The proper approach is first to study the Scriptures to discover what God has revealed about the future. We can then measure current events against what the Bible reveals about the future so we can give thoughtful consideration as to whether there is a legitimate correlation (see Matthew 16:1-3; Luke 21:29-33).

We honor God by correctly interpreting prophetic Scripture (2 Timothy 2:15).

TODAY'S BIG IDEAS

- Prophecy can bring special blessings to Christians.
- Prophecy proves God is the true God.
- Prophecy proves the Bible is God's Word and is trustworthy.
- Prophecy promotes evangelism.
- Prophecy can strengthen believers facing adversity.
- Prophecy comforts us in our grief.
- Prophecy proves God will triumph over evil.

TODAY'S TRANSFORMING TRUTHS

- Scripture draws a close connection between *prophecy* and *purity* (Romans 13:11-14; 1 John 3:2-3). Scripture also relates prophecy to living in *holiness* and *godliness* (2 Peter 3:11). Highlight those words—purity, holiness, and godliness! Live accordingly.

- A recommendation: I suggest that we *agree to disagree in an agreeable way* with our Christian brothers and sisters who hold to different views of the debated finer points of biblical prophecy than our own (see Ephesians 4:15).

Day 3

Guidelines for Interpreting Prophecy

Some people claim Bible prophecy should be interpreted allegorically.

The **allegorical method of interpretation** seeks to uncover figurative or secondary meanings of Bible verses.

I once encountered a person who assured me that the "second coming" occurs whenever a person finds God in their heart. Another person told me that references to "hell" in the Bible refer not to a future destiny for the wicked, but rather, to terrible conditions we create during earthly life.

Contrary to the allegorical approach, there is good reason to interpret Bible prophecy literally. Indeed, based on a literal understanding, we can confidently affirm a *physical* second coming of Christ to the earth. ("Every eye will see him"—Revelation 1:7.) We can be just as confident there will be a fiery hell that will be the eternal habitat of the wicked. ("These will go away into eternal punishment, but the righteous into eternal life"—Matthew 25:46.)

The **literal interpretation** of Scripture embraces the standard, common understanding of each word in Scripture.

Bible expositor David Cooper explained the literal approach this way: "Take every word at its primary, ordinary, usual, literal meaning, unless the facts of the immediate context, studied in the light of related passages and [self-evident] and fundamental truths, indicate clearly otherwise."[6]

There are several good reasons for taking a literal approach to interpreting prophecy. Foremost, a literal interpretation is the standard approach used for all languages. The greater part of the Bible—the prophetic portions included—makes perfect sense when understood literally. The literal method also provides a safe check on the subjectively prone imagination of human beings.

It may surprise you to learn that a literal approach allows for symbols and parables in the biblical text. Significantly, these symbols and parables always communicate something literal. (See "Frequently Asked Questions" below.)

A literal interpretation can certainly help us better understand the nonliteral (or metaphorical) statements that sometimes occur in the text of Scripture. To illustrate, we know that God is spirit (John 4:24). This being so, we surmise that the reference to Him as being a "rock" (Psalm 18:2) is not literally true. This term must be understood figuratively. God is a "rock" in the metaphorical sense that He is our rock-solid foundation.

Finally, 2 Timothy 2:15 instructs us: "Do your best to present yourself to God as one approved, a worker who has no need to be ashamed, *rightly handling the word of truth*." The phrase "rightly handling" literally means "cutting straight" in the Greek text. Bible expositor Thomas Constable tells us that elsewhere, the Greek term "describes a tent-maker who makes straight rather than wavy cuts in his material. It pictures a builder who lays bricks in straight rows and a farmer who plows a straight furrow."[7] We can best satisfy the "cutting straight" requirements of 2 Timothy 2:15 by using the literal method of interpreting Scripture.

Confirmation of the literal method of interpretation occurs within the biblical text itself. More than 100 Old Testament prophecies of the Messiah were *literally fulfilled* at the first coming of Christ (for example, Isaiah 7:14; Micah 5:2; Isaiah 53; Zechariah 12:10). Here is a principle to remember:

If you want to understand how God will fulfill prophecies of the future, consider how He has already fulfilled prophecies in the past. As theologian Charles Ryrie puts it, "In the interpretation of unfulfilled prophecy, fulfilled prophecy forms the pattern."[8]

FAST FACTS ON HOW THE BIBLE SUPPORTS A LITERAL APPROACH

Later biblical texts often take earlier ones as literal. For example, Exodus 20:10-11 takes the creation events in Genesis 1–2 literally. Matthew 19:6 and 1 Timothy 2:13 take the creation account of Adam and Eve literally. Romans 5:12-14 takes the fall of Adam and his resulting death literally. Matthew 24:38 takes Noah's flood literally. Matthew 12:40-42 takes the account of Jonah in the big fish literally. First Corinthians 10:2-4 takes the account of Moses literally.

FREQUENTLY ASKED QUESTIONS

How can the literal approach to Bible prophecy be correct if the book of Revelation has so many symbols?

The book of Revelation does indeed have many symbols. But each symbol points to something literal.

A **symbol** is something that represents or stands for something else.

Symbols in the book of Revelation are typically defined within the book itself. The "seven stars" in Christ's right hand represent "the angels of the seven churches" (Revelation 1:20). The "seven gold lampstands" represent "the seven churches" (1:20). The "golden bowls full of incense" represent "the prayers of the saints" (5:8). "The waters" represent "peoples and multitudes and nations and languages" (17:15). Each symbol points to something literal. Insights on other symbols may be found either in Revelation or other parts of the Bible. *Scripture interprets Scripture!*

How can the literal approach to Bible prophecy be correct if Jesus often used nonliteral parables to communicate prophetic truth?

> The word *parable* literally means "a placing alongside of" for the purpose of comparison. A parable is a teaching tool that uses stories. By taking a story and "placing it alongside" a spiritual truth, the process of comparison helps people to understand spiritual teachings with more clarity. *Parables always point to a literal truth.*

Jesus carefully interpreted two of His parables for the disciples—the parable of the sower (Matthew 13:3-9) and the parable of the weeds (13:24-30). He did this not only so there would be no uncertainty about their correct meaning, but to guide believers as to the proper method to interpret the other parables. That Christ did not interpret His subsequent parables shows that He fully expected believers to understand the literal truths intended by His parables by following the method He illustrated for them.

Here are two examples:

1. *The parable of the weeds* indicates the literal truth that the sowing of the gospel seed will be imitated by a false counter-sowing (Matthew 13:24-30). Only a judgment following the tribulation period will separate the "wheat" (true believers) from the "weeds" (unbelievers or false believers).

2. *The parable of the mustard seed* indicates the literal truth that God's spiritual kingdom had an almost imperceptible beginning (like a tiny mustard seed). But it will grow to be

very large in the world by the time of the second coming (Matthew 13:31-32).

Here is something to think about:

> By explicitly identifying *parables* (Matthew 13:3) and *allegories* (Galatians 4:24) within the biblical text, the Bible shows that the ordinary meaning is literal.

What rules of interpretation can guide us as we seek the correct understanding of prophecy?

Six interpretive rules are essential:

1. Beware of any preexisting personal theological biases you may have. Don't forget that Scripture alone is authoritative.

2. Pay close attention to the context. No Bible verse should be interpreted in isolation from other verses.

3. Different genres of biblical literature have unique characteristics. In the Bible, there are historical books (such as Acts), dramatic epics (Job), poetry (Psalms), wise sayings (Proverbs), and apocalyptic books (Daniel and Revelation). Each genre has unique characteristics. (Both poetry and apocalyptic books, for example, contain some symbols.) Genre-awareness helps us to interpret Bible books correctly.

4. Consult history and culture. The more we understand the biblical world, the easier it is to interpret Bible verses.

5. Pay attention to the "law of double reference." A single prophetic scripture may refer to two events separated by a period of time. Both prophesied events blend into one picture, masking the intervening time period between them. While the time gap may not be clear in the text, it becomes evident in consultation with other verses.

Zechariah 9:9-10 is an example: it prophesies both the first and second comings of Christ.

6. Watch for insights about Jesus. From beginning to end—from Genesis to Revelation—the Bible is a Jesus book (John 5:39-40; Luke 24:27, 44). To illustrate, Jesus is involved in the rapture (1 Thessalonians 4:13-17) and the second coming (Revelation 19:11-21), as well as the future judgments of Christians (2 Corinthians 5:10) and unbelievers (Revelation 20:11-15). To correctly understand Bible prophecy, always watch for how Jesus is involved.

TODAY'S BIG IDEAS

- Always seek to handle God's Word accurately.

- Because prophecies in the past found literal fulfillment, we may expect that prophecies of the future will likewise find literal fulfillment.

- A literal approach allows for symbols and parables—both of which point to literal truths.

- Following the rules of interpretation will keep us on the right path.

TODAY'S TRANSFORMING TRUTHS

- Because the Bible is a Jesus book, let's allow our hearts to be edified by learning more and more about Him as we study Bible prophecy.

- Martin Luther said, "The Bible is alive; it speaks to me." Don't treat the Bible as a dead book with no relevance! It truly is alive (Hebrews 4:12).

- Dwight L. Moody said this about the Bible: "The newspaper tells us what *has* taken place, but this Book tells us what *will* take place."[9] Because the Bible tells us what *will* take place, let us live with a strong sense of anticipation.

Day 4

God's Prophetic Covenants

During Bible times, nations made covenants with other nations in the form of treaties or alliances (1 Samuel 11:1). Individual people also made covenants with each other (Genesis 21:27). Many of these were friendship pacts (1 Samuel 18:3-4).

Occasionally, a person might make a covenant with himself. An example is Job: "I made a covenant with my eyes not to look with lust at a young woman" (Job 31:1 NLT). He purposefully engineered this covenant to help him avoid sin.

Our focus in this chapter relates to the covenants God made with His people (Exodus 19:5-6). God made covenant promises to Noah (Genesis 9:8-17), Abraham (Genesis 15:12-21; 17:1-14), the Israelites at Mount Sinai (Exodus 19:5-6), David (2 Samuel 7:13; 23:5), and God's people in the new covenant (Hebrews 8:6-13). *God is a God of promises.*

A **covenant** is a promissory agreement between two parties.

There were two kinds of covenants during Bible times—conditional and unconditional.

A **conditional covenant** is a covenant with an "if" attached. Conditions were required for the promises to be fulfilled.

A conditional covenant between God and human beings required that human beings meet certain conditions before God was obligated to fulfill what He promised. Such a covenant might be as simple as this: "Obey Me (*condition*), and I will bless you (*promise*)." If God's people did not meet the conditions, God was under no obligation to fulfill His promises.

> An **unconditional covenant** did not depend on conditions for its fulfillment—*there were no "ifs" attached.*

An unconditional covenant between God and human beings involved God's firm and inviolable promises apart from any merit (or lack thereof) of the human beings to whom God made the promises. This type of covenant is also known as a *unilateral covenant* because only one party (God) is making the promises. Others prefer the term *one-sided covenant* or *divine commitment covenant.*

Three of the most important covenants in the Bible that God made with human beings are:

1. the Abrahamic covenant,
2. the Davidic covenant,
3. and the new covenant.

The Abrahamic and Davidic covenants have relevance for the prophetic future of Israel—though Gentiles end up getting blessed as well. The new covenant has both present and future prophetic relevance for all believers, both Jews and Gentiles. We'll consider some details below.

FAST FACTS ON THE ABRAHAMIC COVENANT

God made a covenant with Abraham (Genesis 12:1-3; 15:18-21). He promised Abraham and his descendants that He would make them into a great nation (12:2). He promised to bless Abraham and make his name great (12:2). He also promised, "I will bless those who bless you, and him who dishonors you I will curse" (12:3). He even promised that all the people on earth would be blessed through Abraham

(12:3). Of special relevance to prophecy, God promised Abraham and his descendants the Promised Land (12:1; 15:18-21).

God's covenant promises to Abraham were *unconditional.* They did not depend on any merit (or lack thereof) on Abraham's part.

The land promises will find their ultimate fulfillment in Christ's millennial kingdom, which will follow the second coming. This means the fulfillment will come thousands of years after God first gave the promise. But God is faithful. Israel will possess the land, just as God said!

FAST FACTS ON THE DAVIDIC COVENANT

God promised that one of David's descendants would rule forever (2 Samuel 7:12-13; 22:51). Like the Abrahamic covenant, the Davidic covenant is *unconditional.* It did not depend on any merit (or lack thereof) on David's part.

This covenant features three notable words: *throne, house,* and *kingdom*—words that point to a royal dynasty. This covenant finds its ultimate fulfillment in the royal person of Jesus Christ—the royal King of kings—who was born from the line of David (Matthew 1:1).

Christ will rule as King on the throne of David in Jerusalem during the future millennial kingdom (Ezekiel 36:1-12; Micah 4:1-5; Zephaniah 3:14-20; Zechariah 14:1-21). This reign will extend beyond the Jews to include the Gentile nations. His dominion will reach "from sea to sea...to the ends of the earth!" (Psalm 72:8). "All peoples, nations, and languages" will serve him (Daniel 7:14).

FAST FACTS ON THE NEW COVENANT

In the new covenant, God promised to provide for the forgiveness of sins based entirely on the sacrificial death and resurrection of Jesus Christ (Jeremiah 31:31-34). The new covenant is unconditional. There are no conditions attached to it.

When Jesus ate the Passover meal with His disciples in the upper room, He spoke of "the new covenant between God and his people—an agreement confirmed with my blood, which is poured out as a sacrifice for you" (Luke 22:20 NLT). Jesus did everything necessary for our forgiveness through His once-and-for-all sacrifice on the cross.

FREQUENTLY ASKED QUESTIONS

How can we be sure the Abrahamic covenant was unconditional?

According to ancient custom, the two parties of a conditional covenant would divide an animal into two equal parts and then walk between the two parts, showing that each was responsible for fulfilling the obligations of the covenant (Jeremiah 34:18-19). However, with the Abrahamic covenant, God alone passed between the parts after God put Abraham into a deep sleep (Genesis 15:12, 17). This shows that God made unconditional promises to Abraham in this covenant.

Were there any Jews during the first century who recognized that Jesus would fulfill the Davidic covenant?

Yes. Prior to Jesus' birth in Bethlehem, the angel Gabriel appeared to Mary and informed her, "The Lord God will give to him the throne of his father David, and he will reign over the house of Jacob forever, and of his kingdom there will be no end" (Luke 1:32-33). Notice the three significant words in this passage—*throne, house,* and *kingdom.* Gabriel's words must have immediately brought these Old Testament promises to mind for Mary, a devout young Jew. Gabriel's words were a clear announcement that the babe in her womb would fulfill the Davidic covenant. Her baby would one day rule on the throne of David in the future kingdom. Gabriel's words were full of prophetic anticipation.

How are the promises in the Abrahamic and Davidic covenants reflected in Matthew's genealogy?

The Jews to whom the book of Matthew was addressed were looking forward to the messianic kingdom. They were eagerly awaiting the long-prophesied King who would appear and reign from the Davidic throne.

Significantly, Matthew began his Gospel by pointing to the Abrahamic and Davidic covenants. He opened with these words: "The book of the genealogy of Jesus Christ, the son of David, the son of Abraham" (Matthew 1:1). By beginning his Gospel with the mention of David and Abraham, Matthew was calling attention to the fact that Jesus came to fulfill the unconditional covenants God made with these two.

How do we know God will fulfill all these promises to Abraham and David?

God is a promise keeper! Numbers 23:19 asserts, "God is not man, that he should lie, or a son of man, that he should change his mind. Has he said, and will he not do it? Or has he spoken, and will he not fulfill it?" Deuteronomy 7:9 likewise affirms, "The LORD your God is God, the faithful God who keeps covenant and steadfast love with those who love him and keep his commandments, to a thousand generations."

An aged Joshua declared, "Not one word of all the good promises that the LORD had made to the house of Israel had failed; all came to pass" (Joshua 21:45). He later affirmed, "Not one word has failed of all the good things that the LORD your God promised concerning you. All have come to pass for you; not one of them has failed" (23:14).

Solomon later likewise proclaimed, "Blessed be the LORD who has given rest to his people Israel, according to all that he promised. Not one word has failed of all his good promise, which he spoke by Moses his servant" (1 Kings 8:56).

God truly is faithful! He will fulfill all His covenant promises. These covenant promises are foundational to the prophetic future. We will see this confirmed and illustrated in the chapters to come.

TODAY'S BIG IDEAS

- A covenant is an agreement between two parties.

- God's land promise to Israel in the unconditional Abrahamic covenant will be fulfilled in Christ's future millennial kingdom, which will follow the second coming.

- God's throne promise in the unconditional Davidic covenant will be fulfilled when Christ rules on David's throne in the future millennial kingdom.

- Our forgiveness of sins is based entirely on the new covenant, yet another unconditional covenant.

- God is a promise keeper, so you can count on God fulfilling all of these promises.

TODAY'S TRANSFORMING TRUTHS

- Drive the stake into the ground today. Choose to trust *without hesitation* that God will fulfill all that He has promised in prophetic Scripture. Let there be no doubts (1 Kings 8:56).

- Just as Christ will reign on the throne of David in the millennial kingdom, so He must also reign upon the throne of our hearts. Hold nothing back. Refuse all compromises. He must reign supreme over every area of our lives (John 14:23-24).

Day 5

God's Purpose
for the Present Age

You and I are privileged to live in the church age.

> The **church age** is an extended time that ranges from the day of Pentecost (Acts 2) until the rapture (1 Thessalonians 4:13-18).

It is called the church age because *the church is on the earth* during this time. The church was not on earth before Pentecost, nor will it be on earth following the rapture. Jesus alluded to the church age in Matthew 16:18 when He said, "I will build my church."

> The **church**—or, more specifically, the "universal church"— was born on the day of Pentecost. It is the ever-enlarging body of born-again believers worldwide who comprise the "body of Christ" over whom Jesus Christ reigns as Lord. This universal church is distinct from local churches. There is one *universal church*, but countless *local churches* around the world where members of the universal church meet to worship.

Some Christians claim that the church is just a continuation of Old Testament Israel. However, the New Testament portrays the church as new, and clearly distinguishes between Israel and the church:

1. Jesus said He "will build" His church (future tense) (Matthew 16:18).

2. First Corinthians 10:32 clearly distinguishes between "Jews" and "the church of God."

3. Every single believer in the church age is baptized into the body of Christ (1 Corinthians 12:13). Since this first occurred on the day of Pentecost, the church must have begun on this day (Acts 2; see also 11:15-16).

4. The church is called a "mystery" that was not revealed to past generations (during Old Testament times), but was revealed for the first time in the New Testament era (Ephesians 3:3-5, 9; Colossians 1:26-27).

5. The church is built on the foundation of Christ's resurrection, meaning that the church could not have existed before Jesus' resurrection (Ephesians 1:19-20).

6. The church is called a "new man" (Ephesians 2:15).

We conclude that the genesis of the church was on the day of Pentecost. Ever since then, we have been living in the church age—which, as noted previously, will last until the church is raptured off the earth before the tribulation period (1 Thessalonians 4:13-17; 1 Corinthians 15:50-58).

God has a specific purpose for the church during this current age. Members of the church are called to be Christ's witnesses (Luke 24:45-49; Acts 1:7-8), build up the body of Christ (Ephesians 4:11-13), do good to all people (Galatians 6:10; Titus 3:14), exercise spiritual gifts (Romans 12:6-8), financially support God's work (1 Corinthians 16:1-3), help brothers and sisters in need (1 John 3:16-18), love each other (Hebrews 13:1-3, 16), make disciples of all nations (Matthew 28:19-20), offer hospitality to each other (1 Peter 4:9-11), and preach the Word of God (Mark 16:15-16; 1 Timothy 4:6, 13). Many local churches may fail in one or more of these tasks, but this is nevertheless God's calling on the church.

What about Israel in the current age? Israel is presently in a state of spiritual blindness. The backdrop is that the Davidic kingdom (2 Samuel 7:8-14) had been offered to the Jewish people by Jesus (Matthew 11–12). However, the Jewish leaders rejected Jesus and claimed He performed miracles using the power of Satan. This was a vile accusation. Jesus did miracles in the power of the Holy Spirit, but the Jewish leaders insisted that He was doing these miracles in the power of the *unholy* spirit—Satan. This accusation constituted a decisive turning away from Jesus as the Jewish Messiah. God therefore inflicted judicial blindness and hardening upon Israel as a divine judgment (Romans 11:25).

This, in turn, resulted in a delay of the fulfillment of God's kingdom promises to Israel. These promises have now been postponed until Christ's future millennial kingdom, which will follow the second coming (Matthew 11–12).

God will not lift this judicial blindness until the end of the tribulation period. God's goal is to make the Jews jealous of His offer of salvation. He has done this by opening the gospel to the Gentiles ever since the first century AD (Romans 11:11). With the Jews no longer in the special place of God's blessing—and with Gentiles now experiencing God's salvation—God is slowly but surely moving the Jews toward repentance. At the end of the tribulation period, the blindness of the Jews will be lifted, and a Jewish remnant will repent and turn to Jesus as their Messiah (verse 25).

Meanwhile, Scripture reveals that Jews who place faith in Jesus during the current age become a part of Christ's church (Ephesians 3:3-5, 9; Colossians 1:26-27). They will take part in the rapture, along with the Gentile members of the church.

Now that we understand this distinction between the church and Israel—and God's purpose for each—let us zero in on some characteristics of the current church age. Jesus provides insights about this in His prophetic parables in Matthew 13.

FAST FACTS ON CHRIST'S PROPHETIC PARABLES

A **parable** is an effective teaching tool. Jesus often told a story relating to real life and used that story to illustrate a spiritual truth. Some of His parables provide insights on the present age.

The Parable of the Sower reveals that during the current church age, the gospel seed will be sown onto different kinds of soil (Matthew 13:1-23). This means responses to the gospel will vary during the current age. Some people enthusiastically receive the gospel and become committed believers. Others make a halfhearted commitment that doesn't last. And still others outright reject the gospel.

The Parable of the Weeds reveals that the sowing of the true gospel seed will be imitated by a false counter-sowing of "weeds" during the current age (verses 24-30). Satan and demons love to promote a false gospel.

The Parable of the Mustard Seed reveals that God's spiritual kingdom started very small (like a tiny mustard seed). But it will grow to become very large in the current age (verses 31-32).

The Parable of the Yeast reveals that false teaching will grow exponentially. It will even penetrate the Christian church during the current age (verse 33).

The Parable of the Fishing Net reveals that just as a fishing net can catch both good and bad fish, so there will be both genuine Christians and phony (professing) Christians coexisting within the kingdom during the current age (verses 47-51). Christ will separate them at the end of the age.

The Parable of the Hidden Treasure reveals the incredible value of the kingdom of heaven (verse 44). People should be willing to do anything within their power to possess it.

FREQUENTLY ASKED QUESTIONS

Is apostasy a prophesied characteristic of the end of the present age?

Yes, it is.

> The word *apostasy*—from the Greek word *apostasia*—means "falling away." It refers to a determined, willful defection from the faith or abandonment of the faith.

Scripture prophesies a significant escalation of apostasy in the end times (1 Timothy 4:1-2; 2 Timothy 4:3-4). Even now, apostasy has penetrated the church. Christianity has been "reimagined." Some "Christian" leaders deny God is all-knowing and all-powerful. Some deny that Jesus is the only way of salvation and say Jesus made mistakes when He was on the earth. Some say the Bible is not the only holy book. This issue is so important that I will address it in detail in chapter 7.

Is globalism a prophesied characteristic of the end of the present age?

Yes, it is. And it's already happening. Today's movement toward globalism is setting the stage for the globalism of the tribulation period.

> **Globalism** involves placing the interests of the entire world above those of individual nation-states.

We see globalist policies emerging in economics, banking, commerce and trade, business, management, manufacturing, environmentalism, population control, education, religion, agriculture, information technologies, the entertainment industry, the publishing industry, science and medicine, and even government. The antichrist will ultimately lead a political, economic, and religious union that spans the entire globe. Revelation 13:7 says of the antichrist, "Authority was given it *over every tribe and people and language and nation*."

TODAY'S BIG IDEAS

- The church is distinct from Old Testament Israel.
- God has distinct purposes for the church and Israel.
- Responses to the gospel will vary in the present age.
- False gospels and false teachings will proliferate during the present age.
- There will be genuine and phony Christians who coexist in the present age.
- The end of the present age will be characterized by apostasy.
- The end of this age will be characterized by globalism.

TODAY'S TRANSFORMING TRUTHS

- Let's be active members in our local churches—not simply to receive blessings, but to *give* blessings to others (Romans 12:6-8; Galatians 6:10; Ephesians 4:11-13; Titus 3:14; Hebrews 13:1-3, 16; 1 Peter 4:9-11; 1 John 3:16-18).
- It is wise to daily spend time in God's Word to fortify ourselves from even the slightest hint of doctrinal compromise (Acts 17:11; 1 Thessalonians 5:21; 2 Timothy 3:15-17). The Bible is our sole barometer of truth and our foundation for living.
- Do you personally know any false Christians (bogus believers)? God has called us to evangelism and discipleship (Matthew 28:19-20). What are you waiting for?

Day 6

Israel's Rebirth: A Super-Sign

One of the most significant end-time prophecies related to the current age is that Israel would become a nation again after a long, worldwide dispersion. It seemed like an impossibility. All odds were against it. But amazingly, it has happened.

Israel's rebirth as a self-governing nation in 1948 represented the fulfillment of specific Bible prophecies about an international regathering of the Jews, even though they've not yet trusted in Jesus the Messiah. We might say this is a regathering *in unbelief.* This regathering was prophesied to occur before the judgments that will fall upon the world during the future seven-year tribulation period.

Some 2,600 years ago, the ancient prophet Ezekiel spoke of God's promise to the Jews: "I will greatly increase the population of Israel, and the ruined cities will be rebuilt and filled with people" (Ezekiel 36:10 NLT). God also promised the Jews: "I will gather you up from all the nations and bring you home again to your land" (36:24 NLT).

The **Vision of the Dry Bones** (Ezekiel 37) describes the Lord miraculously bringing scattered bones back together into skeletons, and the skeletons become wrapped in muscles and tendons and flesh. God then breathes life into the bodies. We know this chapter is speaking about Israel, for we read that "these bones are the whole house of Israel" (verse 11). This chapter portrays Israel as becoming a living, breathing nation, brought back from the dead.

Notice that the vision of the dry bones is portrayed as a process:

- dispersed bones form into a skeleton,
- the bones then become wrapped in muscle,
- the breath of life is infused.

The process began before 1948, as Jews from various parts of the world started relocating to the Holy Land. Then the big miracle happened—Israel became a nation again in 1948. The process has continued ever since, with Jews continuing to stream back into the Holy Land from around the world. Ezekiel's prophecy is being fulfilled before our very eyes.

This is significant. In AD 70, Titus and his Roman warriors destroyed Jerusalem and decisively ended Israel as a political entity (Luke 21:20). Since then, the Jews have been dispersed worldwide for many centuries. Even in the decade prior to 1948, no one could have guessed that Israel would soon become a nation again. And yet, it happened.

Ponder this for a moment: While the current regathering of the Jews in the Holy Land is a gathering *in unbelief,* there is a day in the future when there will be a spiritual awakening in Israel (Joel 2:28-29). Armageddon—the campaign of battles that erupts at the end of the tribulation period—will be the historical context in which Israel will finally become converted to Christ (Zechariah 12:2–13:1). It will be quite a day!

Here's what will happen: At the end of the tribulation period, the antichrist's forces will move against the Jewish remnant in order to eradicate them. The remnant will fear imminent annihilation. At just the right time, however, God will remove the spiritual blindness longago inflicted upon the Jews as a judgment, and the Jewish remnant will finally recognize Jesus as the Messiah. The Jews will promptly place their faith in Him.

Israel's spiritual rebirth will include the confession of Israel's national sin (Leviticus 26:40-42; Jeremiah 3:11-18; Hosea 5:15), following which Israel will be saved, fulfilling the apostle Paul's prophecy about Israel in Romans 11:25-27. In dire threat at Armageddon, Israel will plead for their newly found Messiah to return and deliver them (Zechariah 12:10; Matthew 23:37-39; Isaiah 53:1-9), at which point their deliverance will surely come (Romans 10:13-14). Christ will come again at the second coming and destroy the forces of the antichrist.

Later, in the millennial kingdom (which follows the second coming of Christ), Israel will experience full possession of the Promised Land and the reestablishment of the Davidic throne. All this will fulfill the ancient unconditional covenants God made with Abraham and David (Genesis 12:1-3; 15:18-21; 2 Samuel 7:12-13). The millennial kingdom will be a time of physical and spiritual blessing (Isaiah 35:1-10), the basis of which is the new covenant (Jeremiah 31:31-34). *It will be wondrous!*

FAST FACTS ON ISRAEL IN PROPHECY

Ezekiel prophesied that Israel would be reborn in the latter days (Ezekiel 36–37). Israel became a nation again in 1948, and Jews have been streaming back ever since.

Israel will be invaded by a northern military coalition comprised of various Muslim nations and Russia during the end times, likely after the rapture but before the tribulation period (Ezekiel 38–39). God will deliver Israel from the northern military coalition (Ezekiel 39). He will destroy the invaders.

The antichrist will sign a covenant with Israel (Daniel 9:27). This event initiates the tribulation period. The Jewish temple will be rebuilt about the same time (Daniel 9:26-27; 11:31; Matthew 24:1-2, 15, 27-31).

At the midpoint of the tribulation, the antichrist will break his covenant with Israel and make Jerusalem his throne (Daniel 11:40-45). He will also defile the Jewish temple (2 Thessalonians 2:1-4). A Jewish remnant will then escape Jerusalem and be preserved by God in the wilderness (Matthew 24:16-22). This Jewish remnant will trust in Jesus as Messiah toward the end of the tribulation (Zechariah 12:2–13:1; Romans 11:25-27).

FAST FACTS ON HOW ISRAEL'S REBIRTH SETS THE STAGE FOR OTHER PROPHECIES

Israel's rebirth as a nation sets the stage for other key biblical prophecies to be fulfilled both before and during the tribulation period. For example, Ezekiel prophesies that Russia and a group of Muslim nations—Iran, Sudan, Turkey, Libya, Kazakhstan, Kyrgyzstan, Uzbekistan, Turkmenistan, Tajikistan, Armenia, and possibly northern Afghanistan—will launch a massive attack against Israel in the end times (Ezekiel 38–39). Israel obviously cannot be invaded unless Israel first exists as a nation.

The rebirth of Israel is also a precondition to the covenant the antichrist will sign with Israel (Daniel 9:27). How could the antichrist sign a covenant with Israel unless Israel already existed as a nation?

Scripture prophesies the rebuilding of the Jewish temple in Jerusalem early in the tribulation period (Matthew 24:15-16; 2 Thessalonians 2:4). Israel's rebirth as a nation is obviously a precondition to this rebuilding.

Jesus prophesies that the Jews will be forced to exit Jerusalem at the midpoint of the tribulation when the antichrist sets up his headquarters there. Israel's rebirth as a nation is a precondition to the escape of the Jews out of Jerusalem during the tribulation period.

FREQUENTLY ASKED QUESTIONS

Is it possible that prophecies about the Jewish regathering to the land were already fulfilled back in Old Testament times?

No. Contextually, the broader prophecy about Israel's rebirth and eventual attack by a northern coalition takes place in the "latter years" (Ezekiel 38:8) and "latter days" (verse 16). This refers to the end times. Besides, notice that the regathering of Jews is "from all the countries" of the world (Ezekiel 36:24). Never during biblical history had the Jews been delivered "from all the countries" of the world. This event did not find fulfillment until 1948, when Israel became a national entity again, after which Jews from around the globe began coming back to Israel.

Is there demographic evidence that the Jews have been continually streaming back to the Holy Land since 1948?

Yes. When Israel declared its independence on May 14, 1948, the country's population stood at 806,000. By the end of 2005, nearly seven million people were living in Israel, 5.6 million of whom were Jews. Many Jews have continued to relocate to Israel since 2005. Today, the primary motivation for Jews to migrate back to Israel is anti-Semitism, which is now at an all-time high.

TODAY'S BIG IDEAS

- A super-sign of the end times is that Israel would become a nation again after a long and worldwide dispersion. This became a reality in 1948.

- Israel's rebirth sets the stage for many other prophecies to be fulfilled, both before and during the tribulation.

- God still has a plan for national Israel. A remnant of Jews will become believers at the end of the tribulation period.

TODAY'S TRANSFORMING TRUTHS

- If God can restore deeply troubled Israel, then He can certainly also restore you and me when we find ourselves in deep trouble. God can restore us even after we've gone through an extended time of suffering. First Peter 5:10 tells us, "After you have suffered a little while, the God of all grace, who has called you to his eternal glory in Christ, *will himself restore, confirm, strengthen, and establish you*" (emphasis added). Trust God. He's a master of restoration.

- If God can deliver tiny Israel from the massive northern coalition, then He can certainly deliver you and me from the seemingly giant problems we may face. God "is able to do far more abundantly than all that we ask or think" (Ephesians 3:20). God promises each of us, "I will never leave you nor forsake you" (Hebrews 13:5).

Day 7

The Escalation of Apostasy in the End Times

Paul warned the church elders in Ephesus that following his death, false teachers would emerge who would seek to lead church members into apostasy: "I know that after my departure fierce wolves will come in among you, not sparing the flock" (Acts 20:29). He said men would arise "speaking twisted things, to draw away the disciples after them" (verse 30).

> Remember, the word *apostasy* comes from the Greek word *apostasia*, which means "falling away." The word typically refers to a falling away from the truth. It depicts a determined, willful defection from the faith or an abandonment of the faith.

As bad as that episode of apostasy was in Ephesus, it does not compare to the global apostasy that will erupt during the end times. First Timothy 4:1-2 warns: "The Spirit expressly says that in later times some will depart from the faith by devoting themselves to deceitful spirits and teachings of demons, through the insincerity of liars whose consciences are seared." Satan's fallen angels will be working overtime disseminating false doctrine through the mouths of false teachers.

Second Timothy 4:3-4 likewise warns us: "The time is coming when people will not endure sound teaching, but having itching ears they will accumulate for themselves teachers to suit their own passions, and will turn away from listening to the truth and wander off into myths." Who can doubt that these words describe the very days during which we live? As one channel surfs on television in the evening, one witnesses multiple false teachers espousing doctrines that appeal to people's passions, such as the health and wealth gospel.

It's crucial to recognize that falling away from truth often has moral consequences. Apostates do not live the way God desires them to. They often fall into immorality.

> **Moral apostasy** involves a falling away from morality. It refers to the moral decadence that typically emerges among those who fall away from God and His Word.

Second Timothy 3:1-5, 8 provides some specifics regarding the moral apostasy that results from doctrinal apostasy:

> Understand this, that in the last days there will come times of difficulty. For people will be lovers of self, lovers of money, proud, arrogant, abusive, disobedient to their parents, ungrateful, unholy, heartless, unappeasable, slanderous, without self-control, brutal, not loving good, treacherous, reckless, swollen with conceit, lovers of pleasure rather than lovers of God, having the appearance of godliness, but denying its power. Avoid such people...Just as Jannes and Jambres opposed Moses, so these men also oppose the truth, men corrupted in mind and disqualified regarding the faith.

Scripture reveals that apostasy is typically encouraged by false teachers (Matthew 24:11; Galatians 2:4) and escalates during times of trial (Matthew 24:9-10; Luke 8:13). This is prophetically significant, for the future tribulation period will be a severe time of trial, during which false teachers will proliferate. There will be a massive rebellion against God's truth (2 Thessalonians 2:3).

FAST FACTS ON APOSTASY IN AMERICA

Apostasy is entrenched in America today. For example, the *unchurched* in America—over 150 million Americans—are better categorized as "de-churched." They used to be church members, but now they've departed from the faith community altogether.

Some 59 percent of Americans between the ages of 15 and 29 have disconnected from church life.[10] Religious activities, including participating in any kind of religious small group, reading the Bible, and even praying, have declined significantly over the past decade. Colleges provide our young people with all the reasons they need to reject the Bible, Christianity, and "extremist" Christian morality.

Many leave the Christian church because they believe it to be restrictive, overprotective, judgmental regarding sexual issues, unfriendly to doubters, and antagonistic to science. One-third of college-aged adults want nothing whatsoever to do with religion.[11]

The Bible has been so marginalized in American society that it plays little role. As each year passes, the percentage of Christians who believe the Bible is just another book written by human beings increases. Americans no longer view the Bible as a guide for living a meaningful life.

Meanwhile, not even half of the American public can name the four Gospels.[12] Some say the Bible is "everywhere and nowhere." There are copies of the Bible everywhere. But it is "nowhere" in the sense that it is ignored and left untouched. Many churches have reduced the Bible's place in worship and congregational life.

Most Christians—65 percent—no longer share the gospel with unbelievers.[13] Less than one in five Christians are committed to spiritual development in their lives. (This illustrates moral apostasy.)

An increasing number of pastors are defecting from the faith. There are internet websites designed to help pastors and Christian leaders adjust to their new lives after defecting from the faith.

Hybrid religious movements continue to form at an alarming pace. Examples include "Christian Wicca" (Christian witchcraft), Christian paganism, Christian spiritism (with Christian psychics), and Chrislam (Christianity and Islam).

Today, the big emphasis is on feelings and affections, not rational thought. People have rejected an evidential and fact-based faith in favor of an experience-based faith. Mysticism is prevalent. Within many churches, we witness yoga, chanting, the use of mantras, and contemplative prayer (mystical prayer).

Furthermore, Christianity is being "reimagined" by many Christian leaders. Such leaders reject the idea that Jesus is the only way to salvation. They believe everyone is automatically saved unless they purposefully "opt out" of God's offer of salvation.

As bad as all this is, apostasy will explode geometrically once the rapture of the church occurs.

FREQUENTLY ASKED QUESTIONS

Are there examples in the Bible that reveal the terrible consequences of apostasy, and therefore serve as a warning to us?

Yes. Apostasy was a constant problem among the ancient Jews (Joshua 22:22; 2 Chronicles 33:19; Jeremiah 2:19; 5:6). Their apostasy resulted in the Jews going into exile—the Assyrian captivity in 722 BC and the Babylonian captivity in 597–581 BC.

Judas Iscariot and his betrayal of Jesus for 30 pieces of silver is a classic example of apostasy and its effects (Matthew 26:14-25, 47-57; 27:3-10). He departed from the truth for monetary purposes. Later, in remorse, Judas hanged himself (Matthew 27:5), after which his body fell headlong and "burst open in the middle and all his bowels gushed out" (Acts 1:18).

Another example is Hymenaeus and Alexander, who experienced a "shipwreck" of their faith and engaged in blasphemy (1 Timothy 1:19-20). We can also point to Demas, who turned away from the apostle Paul because of his love for the present world (2 Timothy 4:10).

All these episodes of apostasy are warnings to us. Let's avoid being shipwrecked in our faith!

Did Jesus say anything about end-time apostasy?

Yes. He warned, "Many will fall away and betray one another and hate one another. And many false prophets will arise and lead many astray" (Matthew 24:10-11). He said, "False christs and false prophets will arise and perform great signs and wonders, so as to lead astray, if possible, even the elect" (24:24). Obviously, a counterfeit christ or counterfeit prophet who preaches a counterfeit gospel will always yield a counterfeit salvation, which is—in reality—no salvation at all (see Galatians 1:6-9). That's what makes apostasy so incredibly dangerous.

How do today's cults and false religions illustrate apostasy?

Many cults and false religions that pepper the religious landscape today first emerged out of the Christian church. They started when the leaders of these groups received an alleged "revelation" from an "angel"—which, of course, was really a fallen angel (demon). A classic example is Mormonism, founded by Joseph Smith after receiving a revelation from the alleged angel Moroni. Another example is Islam, based on alleged revelations the angel Gabriel brought to Muhammad. In both cases, a wicked spirit impersonated an angel.

What are some specific ways people can apostatize?

People can apostatize by denying God (2 Timothy 3:4-5), Christ (1 John 2:18-23), Christ's return (2 Peter 3:3-4), the faith (or body of Christian doctrine found in Scripture) (1 Timothy 4:1-2), sound doctrine (2 Timothy 4:3-4), Christian morality (2 Timothy 3:1-8), and authority (2 Peter 2:10). Take a little time to look up these verses.

TODAY'S BIG IDEAS

- Apostasy involves falling away from truth and often has moral consequences.

- There will be a significant increase in apostasy in the end times and it will escalate to a fever pitch during the tribulation period.

- America is already profoundly engulfed in apostasy.

- Some "Christian" leaders today are "reimagining" a kinder and gentler Christianity that redefines God, Jesus, and the gospel.

- There is a massive exodus from the church today—including church pastors who have defected from the faith.

TODAY'S TRANSFORMING TRUTHS

- "Sound teaching" is the goal (2 Timothy 4:3-4). Don't be swayed by strange spiritual ideas—whether from a TV preacher, a bestselling book, or the internet. Test all things against Scripture (1 Thessalonians 5:21).

- It is crucial to guard ourselves against having a "form of godliness" while denying its power (2 Timothy 3:5). *Lord, may it never be!*

- God calls us to contend for the faith once for all delivered to the saints (Jude 3). Let's not be *contentious* Christians; let's be *contender* Christians (see 1 Peter 3:15).

Day 8

The Decline
of the United States

Among the more common topics of debate among Christians today is: *What happens to the United States in the end times?*

Of course, when we discuss this, it is best to *agree to disagree in an agreeable way* with our brothers and sisters who hold to a different view than our own. We ought not to be divided over prophetic issues.

That said, Christians hold two primary viewpoints on the United States in prophecy: (1) Some believe that while the United States is not explicitly mentioned in Bible prophecy, perhaps it is indirectly referred to in various prophetic verses. (2) Others believe the United States is not mentioned in Bible prophecy at all. Let's consider both views:

View #1: The United States Is Indirectly Mentioned in Prophecy. Prophetic Scripture often refers to the "peoples" and "nations" of the world. Perhaps these references include the United States. For example:

- Events in Israel will become a cause of stumbling for "all the peoples" of the earth (Zechariah 12:2-3).
- God will, in the prophetic future, "shake all nations" (Haggai 2:6-7).
- God will be glorified among "all nations" (Isaiah 66:18-20).

Such general passages may include the United States. But they do not tell us anything specific about the role of the United States in the end times.

Land Divided by Rivers. Some see a more specific prophecy in Isaiah 18:1-7, which references a land divided by rivers. The United States is divided by the Mississippi River. Isaiah also says this nation is "mighty and conquering" (verse 7). While this may superficially sound like the United States, the context indicates the nation under discussion is modern Sudan.

Tarshish. Others see the United States in the reference to Tarshish in Ezekiel 38:13. This verse informs us that when a great northern military coalition composed of Russia and various Muslim nations invades Israel in the future, a small group of nations will lamely protest the invasion, Tarshish being one of them. Bible scholars have different opinions on the identity of Tarshish. Some say it is modern Spain. Others say it is Great Britain. Others say it refers to the colonies of Western Europe and the nations that emerged from them—including North America and the United States. Still others say it might represent all the Western nations of the end times, including the United States. I assess that tying Tarshish to the United States is far too speculative, with too little scriptural evidence to support it.

Babylon. Still others suggest that Babylon in Revelation 17 and 18 is the United States. Babylon is described as immoral, excessively rich, and views itself as invulnerable. These characteristics may sound like the United States. However, it can hardly be said of the United States, as it can be said of Babylon, that "in your streets flowed the blood of the prophets and of God's holy people" (Revelation 18:24). Moreover, the United States does not represent a global religion, nor is it in any way a religious system (17:1-6). It's also not located in a desert or wilderness (verse 3). One would have to ignore multiple details in Revelation 17 and 18 to hold to this view.

View #2: *The United States Is Not Mentioned in Prophecy.* The United States is the world's single remaining superpower that also happens to be Israel's principal ally. Therefore, one might expect at least a passing reference to the United States in prophecy. Despite this, many believe the United States is not mentioned in prophetic Scripture at all. How could this be?

Many surmise, with good reason, that the United States may weaken in the end times. We know from Scripture that the balance of power will shift toward the revived Roman Empire, headed by the antichrist, in the end times (Daniel 2, 7). This suggests a possible weakening of the United States. The question then becomes: *How might this weakening take place?*

FAST FACTS ON HOW THE UNITED STATES MIGHT WEAKEN IN THE END TIMES

A possible scenario is that the United States might weaken due to a nuclear attack. While it seems unlikely that a nuclear attack could destroy the entire country, a weapon detonated in a single metropolitan area—such as New York City, Los Angeles, Chicago, or Dallas—would cripple an already fragile, debt-ridden US economy.

Another plausible scenario is that the United States might weaken because of an electromagnetic pulse (EMP) attack. A single nuclear EMP weapon, delivered by a missile to an altitude of a few hundred miles over the United States, where it is detonated, would yield catastrophic damage to the nation. It would severely damage the electrical power systems, all devices that run on electricity, as well as computer information systems—all of which Americans depend on daily. It could take years to recover fully.

Less specific, but more to the point, God may bring judgment upon the United States because of its ever-escalating rise in immorality. That would bring a rapid decline. When a nation willfully rejects God and His Word—turning its back on His moral requirements—God eventually reveals His wrath against that nation (Job 12:23; Daniel 2:20-21; Romans 1:18-28). Those who doubt this possibility should consult the apostle Paul's words in Romans 1:18-28.

God may also judge the United States if it turns its back on Israel. In Genesis 12:3, God promised Abraham and his descendants: "I will bless those who bless you, and *him who dishonors you I will curse*" (emphasis added). Let us not forget that God is a promise keeper. A superpower turning its back on Israel might experience super-lethal consequences.

It's also possible that the United States might weaken following the rapture of the church. The United States will probably be negatively affected by the rapture more than most other countries because there is such a high concentration of Christians here. Following the rapture, people will no longer show up for work; bills, loans, and mortgages will go unpaid; leaders of many companies will be gone; and many law enforcement personnel will no longer be around to keep the peace. Chaos will erupt, and our country may plummet into postrapture paralysis.

FREQUENTLY ASKED QUESTIONS

Will the United States be in league with the antichrist in the end times?

I hate to say it, but it's possible. The antichrist will eventually bring about a global government, and the United States will likely be subsumed into this global empire. Even today, our present government administration seems to be moving us away from American national sovereignty and is open to handling more and more problems globally.

It is sobering to ponder Zechariah 12:3, which informs us that "all the nations of the earth" will one day gather against Israel during the tribulation period (compare with Zechariah 14:2). "All the nations" would certainly include the United States (Revelation 16:14).

It may be helpful to keep in mind that following the rapture of the church, there will not be any more Christians on the earth—including in the United States. This means that Christians who have long supported Israel will have just vanished and gone to be with the Lord in heaven. It is easy to see how a Christian-less United States could align itself with the revived Roman Empire and then join the antichrist against Israel.

Is there historical precedent for the fall of mighty nations?

Yes. And in each case, the nation did not expect its impending demise. Those who lived within these nations believed their nation was uniquely invincible and could never fall. The Babylonian Empire, the Persian Empire, the Greek Empire, and the Roman Empire were the superpowers of their respective periods, and yet all of them fell.

The United States may follow their destiny. Given our country's high prevalence of pornography, premarital sex, extramarital sex, homosexuality, widespread abortions, pervasive drinking and drugs, divorce, the disintegration of the family unit, mockery of the Word of God, the marginalization of Christians, and much more, America is in a dangerous place! Since (1) God is sovereign over the nations, and (2) He is a holy God of judgment, then (3) God may sovereignly judge America in the end times for turning away from Him. Job 12:23 informs us that God "makes nations great, and he destroys them; he enlarges nations, and leads them away" (see also Isaiah 14:24; 46:10).

TODAY'S BIG IDEAS

- Christians have different views about the United States' place in prophecy.

- Some believe there are indirect Scripture references to the United States in prophecy, but the evidence is weak, and there is much speculation.

- Others believe the United States is not mentioned in Bible prophecy and suggest various scenarios about the possible weakening of the United States in the end times.

- One thing is certain: The balance of power will shift to the revived Roman Empire in the end times.

TODAY'S TRANSFORMING TRUTHS

- Ask yourself: *Do I live more like a citizen of earth or a citizen of heaven?* Another way to put it is this: *Am I more worldly minded or heavenly minded?* Our heavenly citizenship ought to always supersede our earthly citizenship (Philippians 3:20).

- I suggest we make a resolution: Resolved, to live my life *below* (while I'm here on this earth) as a faithful citizen *above* (in heaven) (Colossians 3:1-2).

Day 9

Millions Vanish
in the Blink of an Eye

The rapture of the church is a key event in Bible prophecy.

The rapture is that glorious event in which Christ will descend from heaven to earth, the dead in Christ will be resurrected, and living Christians will be instantly translated into their glorified bodies. Both groups will be caught up to meet Christ in the air and taken back to heaven (1 Thessalonians 4:13-17; John 14:1-3; 1 Corinthians 15:51-54).

A literal approach to Bible prophecy supports the idea that the rapture will occur *before* the tribulation period. This is known as the *pretribulational* view. (*Pre* means "before," so *pretribulationism* means "before the tribulation.") In support of this view, no Old Testament passage on the tribulation mentions the church (Deuteronomy 4:29-30; Jeremiah 30:4-11; Daniel 8:24-27; 12:1-2). No New Testament passage on the tribulation mentions the church (Matthew 13:30, 39-42, 48-50; 24:15-31; 1 Thessalonians 1:9-10; 5:4-9; 2 Thessalonians 2:1-11; Revelation 4–18). The church's complete absence from tribulation passages indicates it is not on earth during the tribulation.

Christ Himself promises in Revelation 3:10: "I will keep you from the hour of trial that is coming on the whole world, to try those who dwell on the earth." This period of trial—the tribulation period—is described in detail in Revelation 6–19.

Scripture affirms that the church is not appointed to wrath (Romans

5:9; 1 Thessalonians 1:9-10; 5:9). This means the church cannot go through the great day of wrath—the tribulation period (Revelation 6:17).

First Thessalonians 1:9 affirms that Jesus "delivers us from the wrath to come." The term *delivers* in the original Greek text means "to draw or snatch out to oneself" to deliver one from danger. This refers to the church's rapture before the beginning of the tribulation period.

God's removal of the church from the earth before the tribulation is consistent with God's long history of protecting His people before His judgments fall (see 2 Peter 2:5-9). Enoch was transferred to heaven before the judgment of the flood. Noah and his family were in the ark before the judgment of the flood. Lot was taken out of Sodom before judgment was poured out on Sodom and Gomorrah. The Israelite spies were safely out of Jericho and Rahab was secured before judgment fell on Jericho. So, too, will the church be secured safely—*via the rapture*—before judgment falls during the tribulation.

Scripture reveals the rapture will occur "in the twinkling of an eye" (1 Corinthians 15:51-52). This means the bodily transformation living believers will experience at the rapture will be near-instantaneous.

The rapture is labeled the "blessed hope" in Titus 2:13. It is blessed in the sense that it brings blessedness to believers. The term communicates joyous anticipation. Believers can hardly wait for it to happen.

Scripture also reveals the rapture of the church is imminent.

> The term **imminent** means "ready to take place" or "impending." There is nothing that must be prophetically fulfilled before the rapture occurs (1 Corinthians 1:7; 16:22; Philippians 3:20; 4:5; 1 Thessalonians 1:10; Titus 2:13; Hebrews 9:28; James 5:7-9; 1 Peter 1:13; Jude 21). The rapture is a *signless* event that can occur at any moment (Romans 13:11-12; James 5:7-9).

To illustrate this truth, consider how Christ in Scripture is portrayed as a bridegroom (John 3:29) while the church is portrayed as the bride of Christ (Revelation 19:7). According to Jewish custom in Bible times, the groom would become betrothed to his bride, after which he would go to his father's house to prepare a place to live. He would then return at an undisclosed time to retrieve his bride. Today, the church is the "bride of Christ." Christ, our Groom, is preparing a place for us in His Father's house (in heaven). At an undisclosed time, He will come for us at the rapture and retrieve us, after which He will take us to the place He has prepared in heaven (John 14:1-3). Meanwhile, we are called to live in faithfulness to our Groom (Titus 2:13-14).

FAST FACTS ON DIFFERENT VIEWS OF THE RAPTURE

- **Pretribulationism** says Christ will rapture the church before the tribulation period.
- **Midtribulationism** says Christ will rapture the church at the midpoint of the tribulation period.
- **Posttribulationism** says Christ will rapture the church after the tribulation period—at the second coming of Christ.
- **The pre-wrath theory** says the rapture will occur toward the end of the tribulation period before the great wrath of God falls.
- **The partial rapture theory** says only faithful and watchful Christians will be raptured. Unfaithful Christians will be "left behind" to be purged during the tribulation period.

The pretribulational position is most consistent with a literal approach to interpreting biblical prophecy (see John 14:1-3; 1 Thessalonians 1:9-10; 5:4-9; Revelation 3:10).

FREQUENTLY ASKED QUESTIONS

Why is the rapture called a "mystery" (1 Corinthians 15:51-55)?

In the biblical sense, a mystery is a truth that was unknown to people living during Old Testament times but was revealed during New Testament times (Matthew 13:17; Colossians 1:26). While the concept of resurrection is occasionally found in the Old Testament (Psalm 16:10; Daniel 12:2), the idea of a rapture is entirely foreign to its pages. The rapture is strictly a New Testament revelation.

How does the rapture differ from the second coming?

There are notable differences between the rapture and the second coming. For example, every eye will see Jesus at the second coming (Revelation 1:7), but the rapture is never described as being visible to the entire world. At the rapture, Christians will meet Jesus in the air (1 Thessalonians 4:13-17), whereas at the second coming, Jesus' feet will touch the Mount of Olives (Zechariah 14:4).

At the rapture, Jesus will come specifically to receive His bride, whereas at the second coming, He will come to execute judgment (Matthew 25:31-46). We also know that the rapture will occur in the blink of an eye (1 Corinthians 15:52). The second coming will be more drawn-out, long enough for the antichrist to gather his forces to fight Christ (Revelation 19:19).

Further, at the rapture, Christians will be taken and unbelievers will be left behind to experience the tribulation period (1 Thessalonians 4:13-17). At the second coming, unbelievers will be taken away in judgment (Luke 17:34-36), and mortal believers will be left behind to enter Christ's millennial kingdom (Matthew 25:31-46).

Will babies and young children be raptured?

Christians have different views on this issue. Some believe only the infants and young children of believers will be raptured. They find support from the days of Noah. They reason that infants and young children during Noah's time were not rescued from the flood, but only Noah and his family.

Others believe that all infants and young children will be raptured along with all Christians. (This is my view.) The same theological support for the idea that infants and young children who die go to heaven also supports the idea that they will be raptured. For example, in all the descriptions of hell found in the Bible, we never read of infants or little children there. Nor do we read of infants and little children standing before the great white throne judgment, which is the judgment of the wicked dead and the precursor to the lake of fire (Revelation 20:11-15).

The basis of the judgment of the lost involves deeds done while on earth (Revelation 20:11-13). Infants and young children must be exempt from this judgment because they are not responsible for their deeds. Jesus also said children have a special place in His kingdom and that adults must become like little children to enter His kingdom (Matthew 18:1-14). King David certainly believed he would again be with his young son who died (2 Samuel 12:22-23).

It is not that infants and young children have no sin problem. They do. However, at the moment of death, the benefits of Christ's death are automatically applied to them, and that's why they go to heaven at death. Since infants and young children go to heaven upon death, we can infer that infants and young children will also be raptured before the tribulation period. *There is no plausible reason for insisting that infants and children should be targeted for God's wrath during the tribulation period.*

TODAY'S BIG IDEAS

- Christians hold different views regarding when the rapture will occur. A literal approach to interpreting biblical prophecy supports the pretribulational view.
- A pretribulational rapture is consistent with how God typically rescues His people before His judgment falls.
- The rapture is imminent, meaning it could occur at any moment.
- The rapture is called a "mystery" because it was not revealed during Old Testament times but was revealed for the first time during New Testament times.
- The rapture will occur in the blink of an eye.
- The rapture is a "blessed hope" because it brings blessedness to believers.
- Infants and young children will apparently be included in the rapture.

TODAY'S TRANSFORMING TRUTHS

- *Could today be the day?* We should live with a sense of expectancy that the rapture could occur at any moment (Romans 13:11-12; Philippians 4:5; 1 Thessalonians 1:10; Titus 2:13; James 5:8-9).
- This sense of expectancy should motivate us to pursue purity and righteousness in our lives (Romans 13:11-14; 2 Peter 3:11, 14; 1 John 3:3).

Day 10

The Restrainer's Removal and the Rise of the Antichrist

At the rapture, Christians who have died will be instantly resurrected from the dead. Then Christians who are alive on the earth will be instantly translated into their glorified bodies. Both groups will meet Christ in the air.

An immediate result of the rapture is that the Holy Spirit—who indwells the church—will be taken "out of the way" to make way for the rise of the antichrist. Let's consider the details.

Second Thessalonians 2:7-8 tells us that "the mystery of lawlessness is already at work. Only he who now restrains it will do so until he is out of the way. And then the lawless one will be revealed." Notice the two personalities that are mentioned: "he who now restrains" and the "lawless one." I believe this verse means that the antichrist (lawless one) cannot be revealed until the Holy Spirit (he who now restrains) is taken out of the way.

If the restrainer is the Holy Spirit, then it makes good sense to say that He will be taken out of the way when the church is raptured off the earth. After all, 1 John 4:4 tells us, "He who is in you is greater than he who is in the world." The "he who is in" Christians is the Holy Spirit, who is more powerful than "he who is in the world"—that is, the devil, who will empower the antichrist (2 Thessalonians 2:9).

The word *restrain* in New Testament Greek carries the idea "to hold back from action, to keep under control, to deprive of physical liberty, as by shackling." This is what the Holy Spirit does in our day in preventing the antichrist from arising.

The Holy Spirit is specifically said to restrain *the lawless one* or *man of lawlessness*. The descriptive terms "man of lawlessness" (2 Thessalonians 2:3) and "lawless one" (verse 8) indicate that the antichrist is *full of sin*. First John 3:4 explains, "Everyone who makes a practice of sinning also practices lawlessness; sin is lawlessness." So, the antichrist—the man of lawlessness—is a man of sin. The antichrist "shall do as he wills" (Daniel 11:36), not as God wills.

The Holy Spirit's restraining of the lawless one (the antichrist) is in keeping with His broader work of restraining sin in the world (Genesis 6:3). It is also in keeping with the idea that the Holy Spirit can restrain sin in the believer's heart (Galatians 5:16-17).

Why do I say the restrainer will be removed *at the rapture*? I say this because the Holy Spirit indwells the church. First Corinthians 3:16 tells us, "Do you not know that you are God's temple and that God's Spirit dwells in you?" First Corinthians 6:19 likewise tells us, "Do you not know that your body is a temple of the Holy Spirit within you, whom you have from God?"

It makes sense that if the church is taken off planet Earth at the rapture (John 14:1-3; 1 Corinthians 15:51-54; 1 Thessalonians 4:13-17), then the Holy Spirit—who indwells the church—will be "taken out of the way" at that time. This removal of the Holy Spirit's restraint will allow the antichrist, as energized by Satan, to come into power during the tribulation period.

FAST FACTS ON THE HOLY SPIRIT

The Holy Spirit's work is multifaceted. For example, the Holy Spirit inspired all of Scripture (2 Timothy 3:16; 2 Peter 1:21). When

Jesus' mother, Mary, was betrothed to Joseph, "she was found to be with child from the Holy Spirit" (Matthew 1:18). When Jesus was an adult and got baptized, He immediately "went up from the water, and behold, the heavens were opened to him, and he saw the Spirit of God descending like a dove and coming to rest on him" (Matthew 3:16). A bit later, Jesus affirmed, "The Spirit of the Lord is upon me" (Luke 4:18).

The apostle Paul speaks of "the power of the Holy Spirit" (Romans 15:13). John affirms the Holy Spirit's specific power over Satan: "He who is in you is greater than he who is in the world" (1 John 4:4). The Holy Spirit is called "the Spirit of our God" (1 Corinthians 6:11).

The Holy Spirit actively promotes holiness while restraining wickedness (Genesis 6:2-3; Galatians 5:16-22). He is thus ideally suited to restraining the antichrist until the moment of the rapture (2 Thessalonians 2:7).

FREQUENTLY ASKED QUESTIONS

Is the view that human government is the "restrainer" a viable interpretation, as some Christian leaders claim?

In this line of thought, lawlessness in the world is currently restrained by the enforcement of the law by governments. The antichrist will allegedly one day overthrow human government so that he can work his lawless agenda in the world.

The weakness of this view relates to whether human beings—who make up human government—are strong enough to stand against the antichrist, whom Satan will energize (2 Thessalonians 2:9; Revelation 13:4). Satan is more powerful than humans by a considerable measure, and hence many Bible interpreters reject the possibility of any form of human government restraining him.

Some Bible expositors also point out that both Scripture and modern empirical evidence reveal that not all human governments restrain sin; some encourage it.

Is the view that ancient Rome is
the "restrainer" a viable interpretation, as some
of the church fathers claimed?

Some early church fathers believed the restrainer of 2 Thessalonians 2:7-8 was the Roman Empire. The restraining power was viewed as being embodied in the person of the Roman emperor.

Some of these church fathers suggested that the apostle Paul was purposefully vague about the identity of the restrainer. After all, if Paul explicitly identified the restrainer as Rome, and his epistle fell into the hands of Roman authorities, his statement about Rome being "removed" might have been viewed as an act of sedition.

While this understanding of the restrainer may have made some sense to people living during those days, we can see multiple problems in that line of thinking from our vantage point today. The Roman Empire fell from power in the fifth century AD, and the antichrist is still yet to be revealed. This means that whoever the restrainer of 2 Thessalonians 2:7-8 is, it cannot possibly be the Roman Empire.

There is another explanation for Paul's vagueness that makes good sense. He had apparently already spoken to the Thessalonians about the restrainer. Given this, Paul's brief allusion to the restrainer in 2 Thessalonians 2 would have been understood by the Thessalonians without him having to explain the restrainer in full detail again.

There is a further problem with the Rome viewpoint. The antichrist will be empowered by Satan (2 Thessalonians 2:9; Revelation 13:4). As noted previously, whoever the restrainer is, he (or it) must be powerful enough to stand against Satan. No human being—and no human government comprised of human beings—has the power to restrain the work of Satan. Only God has that power.

A final observation is that Scripture reveals the antichrist will rule over a revived Roman Empire (Daniel 2, 7). It hardly makes sense to say that the Roman Empire restrains the emergence of the antichrist, who himself will reign over a revived form of this empire during the seven-year tribulation period.

If the Holy Spirit will be "taken out of the way,"
will He still be active during the tribulation period?

Yes, He will. He will be "out of the way" in terms of the rise of the antichrist, but He will still be active in various ways during the tribulation period. As Bible scholar Paul Feinberg put it, "There seems to be abundant evidence that the Holy Spirit will be active in the earth during the tribulation period. He will empower His witnesses (Mark 13:11). Evangelism will be more effective than ever (Matt. 24:14; Rev. 7:9-14). It is reasonable to assume that as satanic activity increases, so will the activity of the Holy Spirit."[14]

TODAY'S BIG IDEAS

- The only one capable of restraining the Satan-empowered antichrist is God.

- God the Holy Spirit—who indwells the church and acts through the church—presently restrains the emergence of the antichrist.

- At the rapture, the church will be removed from the earth. The Holy Spirit will thereby be taken "out of the way." This allows for the emergence of the antichrist.

- The Holy Spirit will continue to be active on the earth during the tribulation period in empowering God's witnesses and bringing many to salvation.

TODAY'S TRANSFORMING TRUTHS

- The Holy Spirit can effectively restrain sin in our lives if we walk—step by step, moment by moment—in dependence upon Him (Galatians 5:16).

- The Holy Spirit can also produce abundant fruit in our lives—including "love, joy, peace, patience, kindness, goodness, faithfulness, gentleness, [and] self-control" (Galatians 5:22-23). *I want these things, don't you?*

- A recommendation: Given the importance of the Holy Spirit in our lives, let's seek to not "grieve the Holy Spirit of God" by sin (Ephesians 4:30) or to "quench the Spirit" (1 Thessalonians 5:19). Grieving and quenching the Holy Spirit can only be bad for our spiritual lives.

Day 11

Believers Will Be
Resurrected and Glorified

The apostle Paul affirmed that "our outer self is wasting away" (2 Corinthians 4:16). *Paul is right!* All I need to do is look in the mirror to witness the relentless aging process at work.

The good news is that each of us will one day receive a "body upgrade"—a brand new glorified body that will never age, never get sick, and never die. We will receive these wonderful bodies on the day of the rapture; Christians who have passed away will resurrect from the dead, and those of us alive on the earth at that moment will instantly be translated into our glorified bodies. I can't wait! *It will be awesome.*

One reason we know we will receive these wonderful bodies is that Christ Himself has risen from the dead (Matthew 28:1-15; Mark 16:1-11; Luke 24:1-12; John 20:1-18; Acts 1:3; 1 Corinthians 15:1-4; Colossians 1:18; Revelation 1:5, 18). During the first century AD, there were countless witnesses to the fact that this really happened (Acts 2:32; 3:15; 4:18-20; 10:39-40; 1 Corinthians 15:3-8).

Jesus' resurrection ensures *our* resurrection from the dead. Following the death of Lazarus, Jesus told Lazarus's sister, "I am the resurrection and the life. Whoever believes in me, though he die, yet shall he live, and everyone who lives and believes in me shall never die" (John 11:25-26). To prove His authority to make such a statement, Jesus promptly raised Lazarus from the dead!

On another occasion, Jesus stated in no uncertain terms, "This is the will of him who sent me, that I should lose nothing of all that he has given me, but raise it up on the last day. For this is the will of my Father, that everyone who looks on the Son and believes in him should have eternal life, and I will raise him up on the last day" (John 6:39-40).

This means that even though our mortal bodies may pass away in death, turning to dust in the grave, they will be gloriously raised, never again to grow old and die. The day of the rapture is a day to anticipate. It doesn't matter how long your body has been in the grave. At Christ's command, the bodies of all Christians will be instantly resurrected.

FAST FACTS ON THE MORTAL BODY VERSUS THE RESURRECTION BODY

Our present bodies are perishable. Disease and death are our constant companions. It is a continuous struggle to fight off dangerous infections. We often get sick. And all of us eventually die. It is just a question of time. However, our new resurrection bodies will be raised imperishable (1 Corinthians 15:42). Disease and death will be gone forever. Never again will we have to worry about infections or passing away.

Our present bodies are "sown in dishonor" (1 Corinthians 15:43). The reference to sowing (the body that is *sown*) refers to burial. Just as one sows a seed in the ground, the mortal body is "sown" in the sense that it is buried in the ground at death. "Sown in dishonor" refers to the fact that after death, our lifeless corpses are lowered into the ground, after which dirt is heaped upon them. Our new bodies, by contrast, will be glorious. There will be no more dishonor. Our new bodies will never be subject to aging, decay, or death again.

Our present bodies are weak. From the moment we are born, "our outer self is wasting away" (2 Corinthians 4:16; see also 1:8-9). Our vitality progressively wanes with each passing decade. We often get ill, eventually get old, and our bodies will fail us. By contrast, our resurrection bodies will be supercharged, full of power. We won't need to sleep to relieve weariness or recharge our energy. Never again will we tire, become weak, or become incapacitated.

FAST FACTS ON "TENTS" VERSUS "BUILDINGS"

Paul says that while our present earthly bodies are like tents, our future resurrection bodies will be like stone buildings (2 Corinthians

5:1-4). Paul was speaking in terms his Jewish listeners would have understood.

> ➲ The **temporary tabernacle** of Israel's wanderings in the wilderness was a giant tent-like structure.
>
> ➲ This tent was eventually replaced with a permanent building—**a stone temple**—after Israel entered the Promised Land.

The temporary tent (or mortal body) in which believers now dwell will be replaced on the day of the rapture with an eternal, immortal, imperishable body, much like a stone building (1 Corinthians 15:42, 53-54).

Bible expositor William MacDonald sums up Paul's words about tents versus buildings this way:

> A tent is not a permanent dwelling, but a portable one for pilgrims and travelers...The temporary tent is taken down, but a new, permanent house awaits the believer in the land beyond the skies. This is a building from God, in the sense that God is the One who gives it to us...The believer's future body is also described as eternal in the heavens. It is a body that will no longer be subject to disease, decay, and death, but one that will endure forever in our heavenly home."[15]

We will receive these incredible bodies on the day of the rapture (1 Thessalonians 4:13-17).

FREQUENTLY ASKED QUESTIONS

Will cremation pose a problem regarding my future resurrection from the dead?

It doesn't matter how our earthly body (tent) is destroyed. All that matters is that God is all-powerful, and He *can* and *will* raise what is left of our bodies from the dead (1 Corinthians 15:42-44). Even those who are buried eventually dissolve into dust. So, regardless of whether we become dust through burial or cremation, we can all look forward to a permanent resurrection body that will never again be subject to death and decay.

Why did the apostle Paul say "we groan" in our present physical bodies (2 Corinthians 5:4)?

Our present bodies are burdened by sin, sickness, sorrow, and death. Commentator Thomas Constable put it this way: "We groan because we feel the pains associated with mortality, namely, our physical limitations, sickness, and the increasing disability that accompanies advancing age."[16] More to the point, we groan because our tents show signs of wear and tear. We know it's just a matter of time before our tents fall.

In what sense is the Holy Spirit a "guarantee" of our future resurrection bodies?

> The word *guarantee* was used among the Greeks to refer to a pledge that assured the final possession of an item. It was sometimes used of an engagement ring that acted as a guarantee that a marriage would take place.

The Holy Spirit is a "guarantee" or "deposit" in the sense that His presence in our lives promises our eventual total transformation and glorification into the likeness of Christ's glorified resurrection body (see Philippians 3:21).

How do we know our resurrection bodies will be physical?

We know our resurrection bodies will be physical because Jesus Himself physically resurrected from the dead. We know Jesus' resurrection body was physical for six reasons:

1. Christ's body was missing from the tomb (Matthew 28; Mark 16; Luke 24; John 20).

2. His resurrection body retained the crucifixion scars (Luke 24:39; John 20:27).

3. Jesus' resurrection body was composed of "flesh and bones" (Luke 24:39).

4. Christ ate food following His resurrection (Luke 24:30; 24:42-43; John 21:12-13; Acts 1:4).

5. His resurrection body was physically touched by others (Matthew 28:9; John 20:27-28).

6. Jesus' resurrection body was visible to the naked eye (Matthew 28:17).

We know that our resurrection bodies will be like His resurrection body, for Christ "will transform our lowly body to be like his glorious body" (Philippians 3:21). John affirmed, "We know that when he appears we shall be like him" (1 John 3:2). *Our body upgrades will be awesome.*

TODAY'S BIG IDEAS

- Jesus' resurrection from the dead guarantees our future resurrection from the dead.

- Our resurrected/glorified bodies will be imperishable and strong—like a building.

- Our resurrected/glorified bodies will be ageless, painless, and deathless.

- Our resurrected/glorified bodies will be physical.

- We will receive these awesome bodies on the day of the rapture.

- Meanwhile, the Holy Spirit is our guarantee of our future resurrection bodies.

TODAY'S TRANSFORMING TRUTHS

- Whatever physical symptoms we may experience in our present earthly bodies, we can take comfort in the scriptural truth that we will one day receive resurrected/glorified bodies that will be ageless, painless, and deathless. *The best is yet to come* (Colossians 3:1-2; Revelation 21)!

- The apostle Paul addresses resurrection in 1 Corinthians 15. He zeroes in on the rapture starting in verse 50. He then closes the chapter with an exhortation to "be steadfast" and "immovable" (verse 58). May each of us be steadfast and immovable as we await the rapture, regardless of what storms may come during our earthly life.

Day 12

The Judgment Seat of Christ

Christians are sometimes surprised to learn that they will one day stand before the judgment seat of Christ (Romans 14:8-10; 1 Corinthians 3:11-15; 9:24-27). Christ, the divine Judge, will scrutinize each believer's life.

Many Christians have asked me if they can lose their salvation at the judgment seat of Christ. The answer is *no*. This judgment has nothing to do with salvation. Salvation is secure (John 5:24; 10:29; Romans 8:38-39; Ephesians 4:30; 2 Timothy 1:12; Hebrews 7:25; Jude 24). This judgment has only to do with receiving—*or possibly losing*—rewards based on whether one has lived faithfully or unfaithfully during one's earthly life. Even if rewards are lost, the Christian is still saved.

The apostle Paul describes this judgment in 1 Corinthians 3:12-15:

> If anyone builds on the foundation with gold, silver, precious stones, wood, hay, straw—each one's work will become manifest, for the Day will disclose it, because it will be revealed by fire, and the fire will test what sort of work each one has done. If the work that anyone has built on the foundation survives, he will receive a reward. If anyone's work is burned up, he will suffer loss, though he himself will be saved, but only as through fire.

This passage metaphorically describes the possibility of building our lives using bad materials (such as hay, straw, or wood) or good materials (such as precious metals and stones). Notice that some of these materials burn easily while others do not. Hay and straw are the most combustible. Then comes wood. Precious metals and stones are not combustible.

Some of these materials are useful for building while others are not. A house constructed of hay or straw will surely not stand long. It can burn to the ground quickly. But a house built with solid materials such as stones and metals will stand and last a long time. Christ says we should build our lives with good materials.

Bible expositors have wrestled with what might be meant by the various building materials described in 1 Corinthians 3:12-15. Here's my take on it:

> ➲ Gold, silver, and costly stones likely refer to things we accomplish by the power of the Holy Spirit—things we do with Christ-honoring motives and godly obedience.
>
> ➲ Wood, hay, and straw likely represent carnal attitudes, sinful motives, pride-filled actions, and selfish ambition.

Notice the reference to fire in this passage: "Each one's work...will be revealed by fire, and the fire will test what sort of work each one has done" (verse 13). I find it interesting that *fire* in Scripture often symbolizes God's holiness (Leviticus 1:8; Hebrews 12:29). There are also occurrences in the Bible where fire portrays God's judgment upon that which His holiness has condemned (Genesis 19:24; Mark 9:43-48). This leads me to believe that God will examine our works and test them against the fire of His holiness.

This judgment apparently occurs immediately after the rapture, when all believers are taken into heaven (John 14:1-3; 1 Corinthians 15:51-54; 1 Thessalonians 4:13-17). I say this because in the early part of the tribulation period, the 24 elders in heaven seem to represent believers—and they are portrayed as already wearing crowns (Revelation 4:1, 10). This must mean they've previously faced the judgment seat of Christ (after the rapture), for crowns are bestowed at this judgment (1 Corinthians 9:25; 2 Timothy 4:8; James 1:12; 1 Peter 5:4; Revelation 2:10).

This judgment is probably intended to be both an encouragement and a warning. It is an **encouragement** to those who are consistently serving Christ with good motives. It is a **warning** to those who have fallen into carnal living. God will render perfect justice in the end.

Following the judgment seat of Christ is the marriage of the Lamb. Christ is the divine Bridegroom (Matthew 9:15; 22:2-14; 25:1-13; Mark 2:19-20; Luke 5:34-35; 14:15-24; John 3:29), while the church is the bride (2 Corinthians 11:2). Christ claims His bride at the rapture. After the rapture—and after individual Christians have faced Christ at the judgment seat of Christ—a wonderful wedding ceremony will take place in heaven. The church, or bride, is portrayed as now being dressed in white linen (Revelation 19:8). *It will be a sight to behold!*

FAST FACTS ON OUR ACCOUNTABILITY TO GOD

Consulting the whole of Scripture leads me to believe that our judgment will be comprehensive. We will be held accountable for how we used our God-given talents and abilities (1 Corinthians 12:4-7; 2 Timothy 1:6; 1 Peter 4:10), how we spent our time (Ephesians 5:15-16; Colossians 4:5; 1 Peter 1:17), how we treated other people (Matthew 10:41-42; Hebrews 6:10), and our hospitality to strangers (Matthew 25:35-36; Luke 14:12-14).

We will give an account for how we responded to mistreatment (Matthew 5:11-12; Mark 10:29-30; Luke 6:27-28, 35; Romans 8:18; 2 Corinthians 4:17; 1 Peter 4:12-13), our efforts toward winning souls for Christ (1 Thessalonians 2:19-20), and our attitude toward money (Matthew 6:1-4; 1 Timothy 6:17-19).

We will certainly be held responsible for our actions during earthly life: "You will render to a man according to his work" (Psalm 62:12).

"Whatever good anyone does, this he will receive back from the Lord" (Ephesians 6:7-8).

We will also be held responsible for our thoughts and motives: "I the LORD search the heart and test the mind, to give every man according to his ways, according to the fruit of his deeds" (Jeremiah 17:10). God "will bring to light the things now hidden in darkness and will disclose the purposes of the heart" (1 Corinthians 4:5).

We will even have to give an account for our words: "I tell you, on the day of judgment people will give account for every careless word they speak, for by your words you will be justified, and by your words you will be condemned" (Matthew 12:36-37).

The very character of each Christian's life and service will be laid bare under the unerring and omniscient vision of Christ, whose eyes are "like a flame of fire" (Revelation 1:14). This serves as a powerful motivation to submit to Christ in all areas of our lives.

FREQUENTLY ASKED QUESTIONS

What kind of rewards will believers receive at the judgment seat of Christ?

Scripture often speaks of the rewards Christians will receive at the judgment in terms of crowns that they will wear. These crowns symbolize various spheres of achievement in the Christian life:

- *The crown of life* is given to those who persevere under trial, especially those who suffer to the point of death (James 1:12; Revelation 2:10).

- *The crown of glory* is given to those who faithfully and sacrificially minister God's Word to the flock (1 Peter 5:4).

- *The crown incorruptible* is given to those who win the race of temperance and self-control (1 Corinthians 9:25).

- *The crown of righteousness* is given to those who long for the second coming of Christ (2 Timothy 4:8).

Is it possible that some Christians may be ashamed standing at the judgment seat of Christ?

I hate to say it, but *yes*. Some Christians live a carnal lifestyle and may subsequently experience a sense of shame and embarrassment at the judgment seat of Christ. Such Christians may forfeit rewards that could have been theirs had they been faithful. This is implied in 2 John 8, where John urges, "Watch yourselves, so that you may not lose what we have worked for, but may win a full reward."

How can we be happy throughout eternity if we don't fare well at the judgment seat of Christ?

While some will not fare as well as others at the judgment seat of Christ (2 John 8), we must keep this judgment in perspective. Christ's coming for us at the rapture and the prospect of living eternally with Him is something that should give each of us joy. And our joy will last for all eternity. An analogy for this is that some high school students may fare better than others in terms of their grades, but they're all thrilled when they graduate. All are thankful for the future that lies ahead.

My late friend Norman Geisler once told me that in heaven, "all of our 'cups' will be 'running over,' but some cups will be larger than others." Perhaps the most important thing to ponder is that each one of us will be able to perpetually and forever "proclaim the excellencies of him who called you out of darkness into his marvelous light" (1 Peter 2:9).

TODAY'S BIG IDEAS

- All Christians will appear at the judgment seat of Christ.

- This judgment has nothing to do with whether one remains saved.

- Christians will either receive rewards or lose them, based on how they lived after becoming a Christian.

- Things we do with Christ-honoring motives and godly obedience will be rewarded.

- Carnal attitudes, sinful motives, pride-filled actions, and selfish ambition may lead to a loss of rewards.

- This judgment takes place following the rapture.

- Following this is the marriage of the Lamb.

TODAY'S TRANSFORMING TRUTHS

- There will be "haves" and "have nots" when it comes to rewards handed out at the judgment seat of Christ (1 Corinthians 3:15). If you are aware of changes that need to be made in your life, *make them today.* God's camera is always filming. We cannot erase old footage. But we can begin filming new footage today.

- Many Christians struggle with a "sin which clings so closely" (Hebrews 12:1). Satan—"the accuser of our brothers" (Revelation 12:10)—loves to heap on the guilt by reminding us of our failures. I urge you to read my book *Spiritual Warfare in the End Times* (Harvest House Publishers). I believe it will help you immensely.

Day 13

Russia and Muslim Nations Invade Israel

More than 2,600 years ago, Ezekiel prophesied that in the end times, the Jews would be regathered from "many nations" around the world (Ezekiel 36–37). Sometime later, he warned, there would be an all-out invasion into Israel by a massive northern assault force comprising Rosh, Magog, Meshech and Tubal, Persia, Cush, Put, Gomer, and Beth-togarmah (38–39). It is fascinating to uncover the modern identifications of these ancient nations.

⊃ **Rosh** is modern-day Russia. There are two primary reasons for making this identification: (1) Rosh is identified as being in "the uttermost parts of the north" (Ezekiel 39:2). Russia is to the uttermost north of Israel. (2) A place known as Rosh—sometimes using alternate spellings such as Rus, Ros, Rox, Rash, Rashu, and Reshu—was very familiar in the ancient world. It was located in the territory that is now occupied by Russia.

⊃ **Magog** refers to the area today occupied by the former southern Soviet republics of Kazakhstan, Kyrgyzstan, Uzbekistan, Turkmenistan, Tajikistan, and possibly even northern parts of modern Afghanistan. This entire area is Muslim-dominated.

⊃ **Meshech and Tubal** refer to the geographical territory to the south of the Black and Caspian Seas. Today much of this area is modern-day Turkey.

> ⮑ **Persia** is Iran. Persia officially became Iran in 1935. Later, during the Iranian Revolution in 1979, the name changed to the Islamic Republic of Iran.
>
> ⮑ **Cush** refers to the territory south of Egypt on the Nile River—today known as Sudan (Ezekiel 38:5).
>
> ⮑ **Put** is a land located to the west of Egypt and is modern-day Libya (Ezekiel 38:5).
>
> ⮑ **Gomer** is another reference to an area in modern-day Turkey (Ezekiel 38:6).
>
> ⮑ **Beth-togarmah** is yet another reference to a region in modern-day Turkey. (Formerly, Turkey was divided into several smaller territories. That is why different terms are used for Turkey in our text.)

These nations will be headed up by a powerful leader named "Gog" (Ezekiel 38:2).

> The Hebrew term translated *Gog* refers to a king-like role—such as pharaoh, caesar, czar, or president. It means "high," "supreme," "a height," or "a high mountain."

Gog will be a czar-like military leader. He will be a man of great stature who commands tremendous respect.

Here's an interesting fact: An alliance between many of the nations mentioned in Ezekiel 38–39 would likely not have made much sense in Ezekiel's day, since they are not located right next to each other. But it makes great sense in our day because the nations that make up the coalition are predominantly Muslim. Islam is a religion that did not come into being until the seventh century AD, long after Ezekiel's time. The Islamic hatred of Israel is a unifying factor among these various nations.

Russia and the Muslim nations will attack Israel because they will want Israel's wealth (Ezekiel 38:11-12). More specifically, they will want Israel's "silver and gold," "livestock and goods," and "great spoil" (38:13). They will fail. God Himself will destroy this massive invading coalition via a fourfold judgment:

1. God will cause a massive earthquake (Ezekiel 38:19-20). Transportation will be disrupted and the armies of the multinational forces will be thrown into chaos (verse 20).

2. Infighting will break out among the invading troops (Ezekiel 38:21). Perhaps God will induce the Russians and Muslims to turn on each other, each suspecting they're being double-crossed.

3. God will cause a massive outbreak of disease, with dead bodies lying around everywhere (Ezekiel 38:22a).

4. God will pour down hailstones, fire, and burning sulfur (Ezekiel 38:22b). Perhaps a powerful earthquake will set off volcanic deposits in the region, thrusting into the atmosphere a hail of molten rock and burning sulfur, incinerating the remaining invaders.

Three biblical truths are especially relevant at this juncture:

1. God is always watchful over Israel: "Behold, he who keeps Israel will neither slumber nor sleep" (Psalm 121:4).

2. God promised the Jews that "no weapon that is fashioned against you shall succeed" (Isaiah 54:17).

3. In the Abrahamic covenant, God promised Abraham, "I will bless those who bless you, and him who dishonors you I will curse" (Genesis 12:3).

Given these three scriptural truths, we may surmise that attacks against Israel constitute an invitation to divine judgment.

God's judgment is comprehensive. After He destroys the invaders, He asserts, "I will send fire on Magog and on those who dwell securely in the coastlands" (Ezekiel 39:6). Destruction may include military targets like missile silos, bases, and radar installations, as well as religious centers, mosques, madrassas, Islamic schools and universities, and other facilities that preach hatred against the Jews. God may directly send fire, or He could bring it about through Israel's (or some other nation's) nuclear arsenal.

FAST FACTS ON THE TIMING
OF THE INVASION

The idea that the Ezekiel invasion will take place after the rapture but before the beginning of the tribulation period has implications for other end times prophecies. For example, the world will be in a state of chaos following the rapture. Since the United States is heavily populated with Christians, the rapture will have a particularly devastating effect on the country. Russia and Muslim allies may well seize the moment, considering it the ideal time to launch a massive attack against Israel.

Moreover, with Christians gone because of the rapture, and with the invading Muslim forces decimated because of God's judgment, the two most prominent global religious groups that would have resisted the emergence of the false world religion described in Revelation 17 will no longer be around. This will make it much easier for the false religion to emerge.

In addition, with Muslim countries neutralized by God's judgment, it will be much easier for the antichrist to catapult himself into world dominion. Keep in mind that Muslims have long intended to bring about a worldwide caliphate with Muslims in control. God will have removed that possibility, having destroyed the invading Muslim armies. This will make it easier for the antichrist to seize his moment and make his move onto the world stage.

Further, with Muslim resistance now at an all-time low because of God's judgment, the Jews will find it much easier to rebuild their temple on the Temple Mount. No longer will Israel encounter a Muslim threat to rebuilding the temple.

Some may wonder how all of this relates to the scriptural precondition to the invasion—*Israel must be dwelling securely in her land*

(Ezekiel 38:8, 11). Many believe Israel *is already* in a state of relative security. The factors leading to this conclusion are Israel's well-equipped army, first-rate air force, effective missile defense system, and robust economy.

FREQUENTLY ASKED QUESTIONS

Is the antichrist the "Gog" of the Ezekiel invasion?

No. The antichrist heads up a revived Roman Empire (Daniel 2, 7), while Gog heads up an invasion force made up of Russia and some Muslim nations (Ezekiel 38:1-6). Moreover, Gog's moment in the limelight is short-lived—it's all over when God destroys the invading force (Ezekiel 39). By contrast, the antichrist is in power throughout the seven-year tribulation (Revelation 4–18).

Why does the term "Rosh" not appear in some modern Bible translations, except as a marginal reading?

The Hebrew word in Ezekiel 38:2 can be taken as either a proper noun—a geographical place called Rosh—or as an adjective, meaning "chief." If it's an adjective, it qualifies the meaning of the word *prince*, so that it is translated as "chief prince."

I believe Hebrew scholars C.F. Keil and Wilhelm Gesenius are correct in saying Rosh is a proper noun referring to a geographical place. The errant translation of Rosh as an adjective, "chief prince," can be traced to the Latin Vulgate, translated by Jerome—who himself admitted he did not base his translation on any grammatical considerations. He resisted translating Rosh as a proper noun only because he could not find it mentioned as a geographical place anywhere else in Scripture. Unfortunately, many of today's English translations follow Jerome on this verse.

That said, this issue is not terribly consequential. If the correct translation is "Rosh," then the invading force into Israel will comprise Russia and some Muslim nations. If "chief prince" is the correct rendering, then Muslim nations alone—with no involvement from Russia—will invade Israel. Either way, *Israel will be invaded by a massive military coalition.*

TODAY'S BIG IDEAS

- A powerful military coalition apparently comprising Russia and some Muslim nations will invade Israel in the end times.
- A likely scenario is that this invasion will occur after the rapture but before the tribulation.
- Gog will lead this military force.
- God will destroy the invading force.

TODAY'S TRANSFORMING TRUTHS

- Just as God is sovereign over *global* circumstances, so He is sovereign over the *local* circumstances of our lives. It is especially important to trust our sovereign God when life throws us a punch and we are unsure why bad things are happening (Proverbs 3:5-6).
- Just as God is watchful over Israel (Psalm 121:4), so He is also watchful over the affairs of our lives. As Psalm 23 puts it, "The LORD is my shepherd; I shall not want...Even though I walk through the valley of the shadow of death, I will fear no evil, *for you are with me*" (verses 1, 4; emphasis added). It is good to start each day with a recognition of this truth.

Day 14

The Antichrist and His Covenant with Israel

The apostle Paul warned of a "man of lawlessness"—the antichrist (2 Thessalonians 2:3, 8, 9). The apostle John described this anti-God individual as "the beast" (Revelation 13:1-10). This Satan-energized individual will rise to prominence during the tribulation period. He'll head up a revived Roman Empire and initially enact a peace treaty (or covenant) with Israel (Daniel 9:27). He'll then seek to dominate the world.

Starting at the midpoint of the tribulation period, the antichrist will double-cross and seek to destroy the Jews, persecute believers, and set up his own kingdom on earth (Revelation 13). He will speak arrogant and boastful words to glorify himself (2 Thessalonians 2:4). He will be characterized by perpetual self-exaltation.

The covenant the antichrist signs with Israel is prophesied in Daniel 9:27: The antichrist "shall make a strong covenant with many for one week, and for half of the week he shall put an end to sacrifice and offering." The signing of this covenant marks the beginning of the tribulation period.

The term **strong covenant** can be rendered "firm covenant" (NASB1995) or "binding and irrevocable covenant" (AMP). The antichrist will apparently solve the Middle East crisis and force all parties—Jewish and Muslim—to get along with each other. It will be a strong covenant backed by the military might of the revived Roman Empire, over which the antichrist will rule. The idea is: *Obey the covenant or suffer the consequences.*

The antichrist will appear to be an imposing person. He will seem to be a genius in intellect (Daniel 8:23), commerce (Daniel 11:43; Revelation 13:16-17), war (Revelation 6:2; 13:2), speech (Daniel 11:36), and politics (Revelation 17:11-12). Satan—the unholy spirit—will energize him for all his work (2 Thessalonians 2:9). The antichrist will also perform counterfeit signs and wonders and deceive many people during the tribulation (2 Thessalonians 2:9-10).

> The **false prophet** will be the antichrist's personal assistant, his right-hand man, his first lieutenant.

The false prophet will seek to make the world worship the antichrist (Revelation 13:11-12). People worldwide will be forced to receive his mark, without which they cannot buy or sell, thereby enabling the antichrist to control the global economy (Revelation 13:16-17). The antichrist will eventually rule the entire world (Revelation 13:7). There will be political, economic, and religious globalism.

The Holy Spirit is presently restraining the antichrist, along with his lawless agenda. But after the rapture—when Christians indwelt by the Holy Spirit will be removed from the earth, and the Holy Spirit is "out of the way" (2 Thessalonians 2:7)—the antichrist will rapidly emerge on the world scene. However, the beast will eventually be defeated and destroyed by Jesus at His second coming (Revelation 19:11-16). His impotence before the true Christ will be clear to all.

FAST FACTS ON THE LAMB VERSUS THE BEAST

The book of Revelation uses the term "beast" for the antichrist and the term "Lamb" for Jesus Christ. Jesus, the Lamb, was slain for sinners, while the beast will be the persecutor and slayer of the saints. "Lamb" calls attention to the gentleness of Christ, while "beast" reveals the ferocity of the antichrist. The Holy Spirit came upon the Lamb (Jesus) in the form of a dove at His baptism, while in contrast, the unholy spirit (Satan) will energize the beast (the antichrist) (2 Thessalonians 2:9; Revelation 12:9).

FAST FACTS ON THE ANTICHRIST'S MIMICKING OF CHRIST

Just as Christ performed miracles, signs, and wonders (Matthew 9:32-33; Mark 6:2), the antichrist will engage in counterfeit miracles, signs, and wonders (Matthew 24:24; 2 Thessalonians 2:9).

Christ will appear in the millennial temple (Ezekiel 43:6-7); the antichrist will sit in the tribulation temple (2 Thessalonians 2:4).

Jesus is God (John 1:1-2; 10:36); the antichrist will claim to be God (2 Thessalonians 2:4).

Jesus causes human beings to worship God (Revelation 1:6); the antichrist will cause human beings to worship both Satan and himself (Revelation 13:3-4).

Jesus' 144,000 Jewish followers will be sealed on their foreheads (Revelation 7:4; 14:1); followers of the antichrist will be sealed on their forehead or right hand (Revelation 13:16-18).

Jesus has a worthy name (Revelation 19:16); the antichrist will have blasphemous names (Revelation 13:1).

Jesus will be married to a virtuous bride—the church (Revelation 19:7-9); the antichrist will be affiliated with a vile prostitute—a false religion (Revelation 17:3-5).

Jesus will be crowned with many crowns (Revelation 19:12); the antichrist will be crowned with ten crowns (Revelation 13:1).

Jesus is the King of kings (Revelation 19:16); the antichrist will be called "the king" (Daniel 11:36).

Jesus was resurrected (Matthew 28:6); the antichrist will experience an apparent or a bogus resurrection (Revelation 13:3, 14).

Jesus will have a 1,000-year worldwide kingdom (Revelation 20:1-6); the antichrist will have a three-and-a-half-year worldwide kingdom (Revelation 13:5-8).

Jesus is part of the Holy Trinity—Father, Son, and Holy Spirit (2 Corinthians 13:14); the antichrist will be part of an unholy trinity—Satan, the antichrist, and the false prophet (Revelation 13).

FAST FACTS ON DISSIMILARITIES BETWEEN CHRIST AND THE ANTICHRIST

One is the Christ (Matthew 16:16); the other will be the antichrist (1 John 4:3).

Christ is the man of sorrows (Isaiah 53:3); the antichrist will be the man of sin (2 Thessalonians 2:3 KJV).

Christ is the Son of God (John 1:34); the antichrist will be the son of perdition (2 Thessalonians 2:3 KJV).

Christ is the Holy One (Mark 1:24); the antichrist will be the wicked one (2 Thessalonians 2:8 KJV).

Christ came to do the Father's will (John 6:38); the antichrist will do his own will (Daniel 11:36).

Christ humbled Himself (Philippians 2:8); the antichrist will exalt himself (Daniel 11:37 NIV).

Christ cleansed the temple (John 2:14-16); the antichrist will defile the temple (Matthew 24:15).

Christ was received up into heaven (Luke 24:51); the antichrist will go down into the lake of fire (Revelation 19:20).

FREQUENTLY ASKED QUESTIONS

Will the antichrist be a Jew?

No. Revelation 13:1 and 17:15 picture the antichrist as rising out of the "sea"—a term Scripture often associates with the Gentile nations. Antiochus Epiphanes, himself a Gentile, typifies the future antichrist in Daniel 11. Hence, it is unlikely the antichrist will be a Jew. The antichrist is portrayed as the great persecutor of Jews during the tribulation period, not as a Jew himself (Jeremiah 30:7; Matthew 24:15-21; Revelation 12:6, 13-14).

Will the antichrist be a Muslim?

I don't believe so. Daniel 11:36 tells us the antichrist "shall exalt himself and magnify himself above every god." He "opposes and exalts himself against every so-called god or object of worship, so that he takes his seat in the temple of God, proclaiming himself to be God" (2 Thessalonians 2:4). No good Muslim would claim to be Allah or as being equal to Allah. Qur'an-believing Muslims would call for the beheading of such an individual.

Muslims also teach that "God can have no partners." Hence, it is impossible to fathom a Muslim exalting himself to deity in the way Scripture says the antichrist will.

Muslims further teach that Allah is radically unlike any earthly reality. He cannot be described using earthly terms. How, then, could a human Muslim claim to be God and be described in earthly terms, as will happen with the antichrist?

Perhaps most important, it stretches credulity to say that a Muslim antichrist will make a covenant to protect Israel (Daniel 9:24-27). Today, many radical Muslims want to "push Israel into the sea" and "blow Israel off the map." There is no way the Islamic people living in various Muslim countries would go along with any Muslim leader who made such a covenant with Israel. The antichrist-Muslim hypothesis assumes Muslims will universally submit to such a covenant. I cannot believe it. Based on a long historical precedent, Muslims would likely react strongly against such a covenant made by a Muslim leader.

In a similar manner, the Jews—fully aware of Muslim animosity and hatred toward them—would never place their hopes of survival and security into the hands of a Muslim. Such a view makes no sense.

TODAY'S BIG IDEAS

- The antichrist will sign a covenant with Israel—and this marks the actual beginning of the tribulation period.
- The antichrist will be a man of lawlessness. The book of Revelation refers to him as a "beast." Satan will energize him.
- The antichrist will mimic Christ, but the dissimilarities between him and Christ are staggering.
- The antichrist will seem to be a genius in intellect, commerce, war, speech, and politics.
- The antichrist will elevate himself to deity and demand worship.
- The false prophet will be instrumental in leading the world to worship the antichrist.

TODAY'S TRANSFORMING TRUTHS

- The antichrist promotes lawlessness. Contrary to his agenda, may each of us honor and obey God's law—not to earn favor with God, but in joyful appreciation for the grace-gift of salvation He has given us (John 15:14).
- The antichrist promotes idolatry. Contrary to his agenda, may each of us worship and honor God alone (1 Samuel 7:4; Psalm 86:10; Luke 4:8).

Day 15

The Rebuilt Temple and
Signs of the Times

The Jewish temple will be rebuilt during the tribulation period.

> **The temple** is a place of worship for the Jewish people and is where God typically manifests Himself to His people.

We know the temple will be rebuilt because Daniel 9:27 speaks of the sacrifices that will be offered in the temple during the first half of the tribulation period. We also know there will be a temple because Jesus, in His Olivet Discourse, prophesied that this future temple would be desecrated: "When you see the abomination of desolation spoken of by the prophet Daniel, standing in the holy place (let the reader understand), then let those who are in Judea flee to the mountains" (Matthew 24:15-16).

> **The abomination of desolation** involves desecration of the Jewish temple by the antichrist, who will set up an image of himself within the temple at the midpoint of the tribulation period (compare with Isaiah 14:13-14 and Ezekiel 28:2-9).

Though the temple is not yet rebuilt, it is highly relevant that preparations are being made during our present day to rebuild it. Jewish individuals and groups—an example being the Temple Institute—have been working behind the scenes to prepare various materials that will be needed for the future temple, including priestly robes, temple tapestries, and worship utensils. These items are being prefabricated so that when the temple is finally rebuilt, everything will be ready for it. Meanwhile, the Jewish Sanhedrin has been reestablished and is now raising money and drawing up architectural plans to rebuild the temple. The fulfillment of this temple prophecy seems to be on the not-too-distant horizon.

The rebuilding of the Jewish temple may be considered a *sign of the times.*

> A **sign of the times** is an event of prophetic significance that points to the end times. These signs will find fulfillment during the tribulation period—but even now, as illustrated by the Jewish temple, we witness the *foreshadows* of these prophecies.

To make the signs of the times more accessible to prophecy students, I have compiled them into six categories: the rebirth-of-Israel sign, moral signs, religious signs, national-alignment signs, earth and sky signs, and technological signs.

FAST FACTS ON SIGNS OF THE TIMES

The Rebirth-of-Israel Sign. The Jews will be regathered from the "four corners of the earth" in the end times after the nation has been reestablished (Isaiah 11:12; 66:7-8). God promised, "I will take you from the nations and gather you from all the countries and bring you into your own land" (Ezekiel 36:24). Israel became a nation again in 1948, and Jews have been streaming back to it ever since. This is a super-sign of the end times because it sets the stage for the fulfillment of a number of other key prophecies.

Moral Signs of the Times. In the end times, "people will be lovers of self, lovers of money, proud, arrogant, abusive, disobedient to their parents, ungrateful, unholy, heartless, unappeasable, slanderous, without self-control, brutal, not loving good, treacherous, reckless, swollen with conceit, lovers of pleasure rather than lovers of God, having the appearance of godliness, but denying its power" (2 Timothy 3:1-5).

Jesus warned of the end times, "Because lawlessness will be increased, the love of many will grow cold" (Matthew 24:12). He also warned that people would constantly be partying it up, unconcerned about God and spiritual matters, just as it was back in the days of Noah (verses 37-39).

Religious Signs of the Times. The end times will be characterized by a rise in false christs, false prophets, and false teachers (Matthew 24:24; Mark 13:22). There will also be a significant increase in apostasy. First Timothy 4:1-2 warns: "The Spirit expressly says that in later times some will depart from the faith by devoting themselves to deceitful spirits and teachings of demons." Likewise, 2 Timothy 4:3-4 warns: "The time is coming when people will not endure sound teaching, but having itching ears they will accumulate for themselves teachers to suit their own passions, and will turn away from listening to the truth and wander off into myths."

National-Alignment Signs of the Times. A "United States of Europe" will emerge in the end times—a ten-nation confederacy that will constitute a revived Roman Empire (Daniel 2:41-44; 7:7, 23-24; Revelation 17:12-13). There will also be an end-time military coalition against Israel that includes Russia, Iran, Sudan, Turkey, Libya, and other Muslim nations (Ezekiel 38–39). Russia already has military alliances with some of these nations.

Earth and Sky Signs of the Times. During the tribulation period, there will be a tremendous increase in the frequency and intensity of earthquakes and signs in the heavens (Matthew 24:7). Luke 21:11 warns: "There will be great earthquakes...And there will be terrors and great signs from heaven." These signs could include strange weather patterns, meteors striking the earth, and a darkening of the moon and other celestial bodies (Revelation 8:10-12).

Technological Signs of the Times. Matthew 24:14 tells us that before the second coming of Christ, the gospel must be preached to every nation. Today's technology—satellites, the internet, global media, translation technologies, publishing technologies, rapid transportation, and the like—makes this possible. Revelation 13:16-17 tells us that the antichrist will wield economic control over everyone on earth. Today's technology—the internet, supercomputers, biometric identification procedures, RFID chips, and smart card technology—makes this possible. Revelation 8:7 tells us that much of the earth will be destroyed by fire. Today's nuclear weaponry makes this possible.

FREQUENTLY ASKED QUESTIONS

Since we are witnessing foreshadows of the signs of the times, can we guestimate the dates of future prophetic events?

It is unwise even to attempt guessing dates! Scripture reveals that no one can know the day or the hour of specific end-time events. In Matthew 24:36, Jesus urges, "Concerning that day and hour no one knows, not even the angels of heaven, nor the Son, but the Father only." He likewise affirms in Acts 1:7, "It is not for you to know times or seasons that the Father has fixed by his own authority."

While date-setting is prohibited, the Lord Jesus indicated that we can infer that His coming is not far off: "From the fig tree learn its lesson: as soon as its branch becomes tender and puts out its leaves, you know that summer is near. So also, when you see all these things, you know that he is near, at the very gates" (Matthew 24:32-33).

What are we to make of the widespread mockery of Christians who believe in the prophetic signs of the times?

Christians are warned in 2 Peter 3:3-4 of the unbelief that will predominate on planet Earth during the end times. We are told that "scoffers will come in the last days with scoffing, following their own sinful desires" (verse 3). They will scoff by saying, "Where is the promise of his coming? For ever since the fathers fell asleep, all things are continuing as they were from the beginning of creation" (verse 4). Jude 18 likewise affirms, "In the last time there will be scoffers, following their own ungodly passions."

Count on it and get used to it: Christians who believe in the prophetic signs of the times will be increasingly mocked and ridiculed for their beliefs! Such is already occurring among a new and more vitriolic breed of atheists and humanists.

TODAY'S BIG IDEAS

- Scripture prophesies the building of a Jewish temple during the tribulation period. Preparations are being made even now for this temple.

- A *sign of the times* is an event of prophetic significance that points to the end times. (The rebuilding of the Jewish temple is an example.)

- Israel's rebirth as a nation is a super-sign, setting the stage for all that follows (including the temple's rebuilding).

- *Moral* signs of the times point to the immorality and lawlessness of people in the end times. *Religious* signs of the times point to false christs, false prophets, false teachers, and the rise of apostasy. *National-alignment* signs of the times point to end-time alliances as well as eventual globalism. *Earth and sky* signs point to the increase in earthquakes and signs in the heavens. *Technological* signs point to how modern technology facilitates the fulfillment of specific prophecies of the end times.

- It is legitimate to infer that we are living in the end times—but let's not fall prey to setting dates!

TODAY'S TRANSFORMING TRUTHS

- Jesus chastised the Jewish leaders of the first century for failing to recognize the signs of those times. Jesus, as the Jewish Messiah, was the fulfillment of multiple Old Testament prophecies (signs), and yet the Jewish leaders were blind to it (Matthew 16:1-3; Isaiah 11; 35). Let's not make the same mistake. Let's learn the signs of the times and resolve to be accurate observers!

- Meanwhile, let us seek to reach as many people as possible with the gospel of Christ, knowing that opportune time to reach them is growing shorter (Matthew 28:16-20).

Day 16

The 144,000
Jewish Evangelists

One of the more controversial aspects of Bible prophecy relates to the identity of the 144,000 who are sealed as mentioned in Revelation 7 and 14.

> **The 144,000** are described as being "from every tribe of the sons of Israel"—12,000 from each of the 12 tribes (Revelation 7:4-8).

Some Bible expositors believe the 144,000 people mentioned in these passages constitute a symbolic description of the church. Those who hold to this position reason that the 144,000 could not be from the literal tribes of Israel because the tribe of Dan is omitted from the 12 tribes, and the tribe of Levi is included. Moreover, Galatians 3:29 tells us that "if you are Christ's, then you are Abraham's offspring, heirs according to promise." Followers of Christ are called "the circumcision" in Philippians 3:3. Followers of Christ are also called "the Israel of God" in Galatians 6:16. Such verses are interpreted to mean that the church fulfills the role of true Israel. This being so, the 144,000 in Revelation 7 and 14 must represent the church and not Israel.

Contrary to this view, the immediate context of our passage refers to 144,000 *Jewish* men—12,000 from *each tribe*—who live during the tribulation period (Revelation 7:1-8; 14:4). That specific tribes are mentioned along with specific numbers for those tribes (12) removes all possibility that this is a figure of speech. Nowhere else in the Bible does a reference to the 12 tribes of Israel mean anything but the 12 tribes of Israel. The word "tribe" is never used of anything but a literal ethnic group.

Interpreting the 144,000 as literal Jewish men makes good sense when the broader context is considered. God initially chose the Jews to share the good news of God with all other people around the world (see Isaiah 42:6; 43:10). They were to be His representatives to the Gentiles. The Jews failed at this task, especially because they did not even recognize Jesus as the divine Messiah. This was nevertheless their calling. During the tribulation, these 144,000 Jews will finally fulfill this mandate. They will be God's witnesses worldwide and there will be a mighty harvest of souls (Revelation 7:9-14).

The witnesses will be protectively "sealed" by God.

> During Bible times, **seals** were used as signs of ownership and protection. These Jewish believers are "owned" by God, and He protects them during their time of service in the tribulation period (Revelation 14:1-4).

These sealed servants of God will apparently be preachers. They will fulfill Matthew 24:14: "This gospel of the kingdom will be proclaimed throughout the entire world as a testimony to all nations, and then the end will come."

The 144,000 will apparently emerge on the scene in the early part of the tribulation period, sometime after the rapture. They must engage in evangelism early in the tribulation because the believers martyred during the fifth seal judgment (Revelation 6:9-11) are among the fruit of their labors. (The seal judgments will take place during the first half of the tribulation period, which tells us the martyrs associated with the fifth seal will die during the first half of the tribulation period.)

FAST FACTS ON THE
144,000 JEWISH EVANGELISTS

There will be 144,000 Jewish evangelists (Revelation 7; 14). These men will be sealed from every tribe (7:4). The Lamb's and the Father's names will be on their foreheads (14:1). The men will learn a new song (verse 3) and will live in purity (verse 4). They are among God's redeemed (verses 3-4). And they will be honest and blameless (verse 5).

FAST FACTS ON THREE COMMONLY MISUNDERSTOOD BIBLE VERSES

Galatians 3:29. This verse tells us that "if you are Christ's, then you are Abraham's offspring, heirs according to promise." This does not mean that distinctions between the church and Israel are thereby obliterated (see 1 Corinthians 10:32). Those who become joined to Christ by faith become *spiritual* descendants of Abraham and consequently become beneficiaries of some of God's promises to Abraham. Though believers in Christ are Abraham's *spiritual* offspring, they remain distinct from ethnic Israel. One must not forget the pivotal teaching of the apostle Paul in Romans 9–11, where he reminds us that God still has a plan for ethnic Israel, as distinct from the church. Galatians 3:29 therefore does not support the idea that the 144,000 "from every tribe of the sons of Israel" metaphorically refers to the church.

Philippians 3:3. Believers in Christ are here called "the circumcision." However, Paul was referring not to physical circumcision (as practiced by the Jews) but to the circumcision *of the heart* that occurs the moment a person trusts in Jesus Christ for salvation. Hence, the verse does not support the idea that the 144,000 "from every tribe of the sons of Israel" metaphorically refers to the church.

Galatians 6:16. The apostle Paul here refers to "the Israel of God." This does not mean the church is the new Israel. Rather, Paul is referring to *individual saved Jews*—that is, individual Jews who have placed their faith in Jesus for salvation. That these individual Jews have placed faith in Jesus does not do away with God's promises to national Israel. Remember that the term *Israel* refers to physical Jews everywhere else in the New Testament (some 65 times). In Paul's writings, the church and Israel consistently remain distinct (see Romans 9–11; 1 Corinthians 10:32). Galatians 6:16 therefore does not support the idea that the

144,000 "from every tribe of the sons of Israel" metaphorically refers to the church.

FREQUENTLY ASKED QUESTIONS

How do all these Jewish men suddenly become believers in Jesus Christ?

These Jews will probably become believers in Jesus in a way similar to that of the apostle Paul, himself a Jew, who had a Damascus-road encounter with the risen Christ (see Acts 9:1-9). Interestingly, in 1 Corinthians 15:8, the apostle Paul refers to himself in his conversion to Christ as "one untimely born." Some Bible expositors believe Paul may have been alluding to his 144,000 Jewish tribulation brethren, who would be spiritually "born" in a way like him—only Paul was spiritually born far before them.

If Revelation 7 and 14 refer to literal Jewish tribes, why was the tribe of Dan omitted?

The Old Testament has some 20 variant lists of the Jewish tribes. Hence, no list of the 12 tribes of Israel must be identical. Most scholars today agree that Dan's tribe was omitted in Revelation 7 and 14 because that tribe was frequently guilty of idolatry and, as a result, was largely obliterated (Leviticus 24:11; Judges 18:1, 30; see also 1 Kings 12:28-29). To engage in unrepentant idolatry is to be cut off from God's blessing.

If Revelation 7 and 14 are referring to literal Jewish tribes, why was the tribe of Levi included—a tribe not included in Old Testament tribal lists?

The priestly functions of the tribe of Levi ceased with the coming of Jesus Christ, the ultimate High Priest. Indeed, the Levitical priesthood was fulfilled in the person of Christ (Hebrews 7–10). Because there was no further need for the services of the tribe of Levi as priests, there was no further reason for keeping this tribe distinct and separate from the others. Hence, they were properly included in the tribal listing in the book of Revelation.

Is there a connection between these 144,000 Jews and the judgment of the nations, which follows the second coming (Matthew 25:31-46)?

Yes, I believe so.

> The **judgment of the nations** will determine which individual Gentiles are believers. They will be permitted entrance into Christ's millennial kingdom.

The nations mentioned in Matthew 25:31-46 are comprised of sheep and goats, representing the saved and the unsaved among the Gentiles. They are judged based upon how they treat Christ's "brothers." These brothers are likely the 144,000 Jews mentioned in Revelation 7 and 14, Christ's Jewish brothers who will bear witness of Him during the tribulation. The 144,000 will find it difficult to buy food during the tribulation because they will refuse to receive the mark of the beast (Revelation 13:16-17). Only true believers (sheep) will come to their aid. The unbelievers (goats) will render them no aid.

TODAY'S BIG IDEAS

- The 144,000 in Revelation 7 and 14 refers not to the church but to Jewish men.

- 144,000 Jewish men—12,000 from each of the 12 tribes— will become believers in Christ and will be His witnesses during the tribulation period.

- They will probably become believers in Jesus much like the apostle Paul did during his Damascus-road experience.

- These men will be protectively "sealed" by God until their mission is complete.

- They will share the "gospel of the kingdom" throughout the world.

TODAY'S TRANSFORMING TRUTHS

- Second Timothy 2:15 instructs us, "Do your best to present yourself to God as one approved, a worker who has no need to be ashamed, *rightly handling the word of truth*" (emphasis added). The King James Version translates the latter part of the verse "rightly dividing the word of truth." This means we must not confuse God's plans for Israel and the church. We must "rightly divide" God's distinct plans for each.

- Just as the 144,000 Jewish evangelists will faithfully share the gospel with any who will listen, so you and I are called to apologetics and evangelism—sharing the gospel with any who will listen (Acts 8:26-40; 1 Peter 3:15; Jude 3).

- Just as the 144,000 are sealed by God, so you and I are sealed by the Holy Spirit (Ephesians 4:30). *We are secure in our salvation.* Rejoice!

Day 17

The Two Prophetic Witnesses

God will raise up two mighty prophetic witnesses during the tribulation period. They will testify of the true God with incredible power—much like the power of Elijah (1 Kings 17; Malachi 4:5) and Moses (Exodus 7–11).

> **Two witnesses** are important. The Old Testament stipulates that two witnesses are required to confirm a testimony (Deuteronomy 17:6; 19:15; Matthew 18:16; John 8:17; Hebrews 10:28).

In Revelation 11:3-6, we read God's prophetic promise:

> I will grant authority to my two witnesses, and they will prophesy for 1,260 days, clothed in sackcloth. These are the two olive trees and the two lampstands that stand before the Lord of the earth. And if anyone would harm them, fire pours from their mouth and consumes their foes. If anyone would harm them, this is how he is doomed to be killed. They have the power to shut the sky, that no rain may fall during the days of their prophesying, and they have power over the waters to turn them into blood and to strike the earth with every kind of plague, as often as they desire.

The clothing of the two witnesses—made of goat or camel hair—is significant (verse 3). Such garments symbolically express mourning over the world's wretched condition and lack of repentance. The reference to olive trees and lampstands symbolizes the light of spiritual revival (verse 4).

The two prophets will minister for precisely 1,260 days, which measures out to exactly three-and-a-half years. Scholars debate, however, whether they minister during the first half or the second half of the tribulation period. Most conclude that the two witnesses do their miraculous work during the first three-and-a-half years. The antichrist's execution of them seems to fit best with other events that will transpire in the middle of the tribulation—such as the antichrist's exaltation of himself to godhood in defiance of the true God and His witnesses. Moreover, after being dead for three-and-a-half days, the resurrection of the two witnesses would make a much more significant impact on the world in the middle of the tribulation than at the end, when Armageddon is in full swing, just before the second coming of Christ.

Once the two witnesses have completed their ministry, God will sovereignly permit the antichrist (the beast) to execute them (Revelation 11:7). Their bodies will be allowed to lie lifeless in Jerusalem. Jerusalem was figuratively called "Sodom and Egypt" because of its inhabitants' apostasy and rejection of God. The description of Jerusalem as being no better than Sodom and Egypt was used to show that the once-holy city had become no better than places that were famous for their hatred of the true God and His Word.

Apparently through the mediums of television and the internet, "the peoples and tribes and languages and nations" will gaze at the dead witnesses for three days. Only modern technology can explain how the entire world will be able to view all of this.

During Bible times, the refusal to bury a corpse was a way of showing contempt (Deuteronomy 21:22-23; Psalm 79:2-3; Acts 14:19). Hence, by leaving the dead bodies in the street, the people of the world render the greatest possible insult to God's spokesmen. It is equivalent to the people of the world collectively spitting upon the corpses.

The world's people will have a "Christmas" celebration—exchanging presents—when the witnesses are executed by the antichrist (Revelation 11:10). They will do this because they are relieved that the two prophetic witnesses are no longer around. Based on biblical history, the only prophets people love are dead ones.

After the prophets lie in the street dead for three-and-a-half days, "a breath of life from God" enters them (verse 11; see also Genesis 2:7). Christmas-like celebrations quickly give way to worldwide fear as the lifeless corpses suddenly stand up in full view of live television and internet feeds. Clips of this event will be replayed repeatedly through various media. It will no doubt "go viral" on the internet. The resurrection and ascension of the two witnesses will serve as a giant exclamation point to their prophetic words throughout their three-and-a-half-year ministry. In my mind's eye, I can picture them resurrecting from the dead and then asking, "Any questions?"

FAST FACTS ON THE TWO WITNESSES

The two prophetic witnesses will prophesy for 1,260 days (Revelation 11:3). Fire will consume any who try to kill them (verse 5). They will have miraculous powers (verse 6). The antichrist will put them to death when their ministry is complete (verse 7). Their dead bodies will lie in the street (verse 8). People worldwide will celebrate their deaths (verses 9-10). They will resurrect from the dead and ascend into heaven (verses 11-12).

FAST FACTS ON THE POSSIBILITY THAT THE TWO WITNESSES ARE MOSES AND ELIJAH

The tribulation period—the seventieth week of Daniel—is a period in which God deals with the Jews, just as He did in the first 69 weeks of Daniel. Because Moses and Elijah are the two most influential figures in Jewish history, it would make good sense that they be on the scene during the tribulation period.

Both the Old Testament and Jewish tradition expected Moses (Deuteronomy 18:15, 18) and Elijah (Malachi 4:5) to return in the future. In addition, Moses and Elijah appeared on the Mount of Transfiguration with Jesus: "He was transfigured before them, and his face shone like the sun, and his clothes became white as light. *And behold, there appeared to them Moses and Elijah, talking with him*" (Matthew 17:1-3; emphasis added). Their appearance to Jesus shows their centrality. Hence, it stands to reason that they might be on the scene during the future tribulation period.

The miracles portrayed in Revelation 11 are like those previously performed by Moses and Elijah during Old Testament times. The two prophets will have the power to prevent rain, turn water into blood, and afflict human beings with plagues (Revelation 11:5-6). Likewise, Moses turned water into blood (Exodus 7:14-25) and afflicted human beings with plagues (Exodus 9:8-12). As a judgment, Elijah pronounced the following words to a sinful, unrepentant people: "As the LORD, the God of Israel, lives, before whom I stand, there shall be neither dew nor rain these years, except by my word" (1 Kings 17:1).

Both Moses and Elijah left the earth in unusual ways. Elijah never died, but rather, was transported to heaven in a fiery chariot (2 Kings 2:11-12). God supernaturally buried Moses' body in a location unknown to other human beings (Deuteronomy 34:5-6; Jude 9).

Given such factors, some Bible expositors suggest God will send two of His mightiest servants back to earth during the tribulation period. We are reminded of how Moses and Elijah rescued Israel from bondage and idolatry during Old Testament times. They may reappear in the tribulation to warn Israel against succumbing to the false religion of the antichrist and the false prophet.

FREQUENTLY ASKED QUESTIONS

Alternatively, is it possible that the two prophetic witnesses will be Enoch and Elijah?

Some Bible expositors think so. Both Enoch and Elijah were upright men who were raptured to heaven (see Genesis 5:24; Hebrews 11:5; 2 Kings 2:11). Neither one of them experienced death. Both were prophets—one a Gentile (Enoch) and the other a Jew (Elijah). For the first 300 years of church history, the church fathers unanimously held that the two prophets of Revelation 11 would be Enoch and Elijah. So, maybe God will ordain one witness to speak to Jews and the other to speak to Gentiles during the tribulation period.

Is it possible that the two prophetic witnesses might be two entirely new prophets?

It is indeed possible! Those who hold to this view reason that the text would surely identify famous Old Testament personalities if they were to come back. Because they are not identified, the two witnesses may be new prophets whom God specially raises up for ministry during the tribulation period.

TODAY'S BIG IDEAS

- During the tribulation period, God will raise up two mighty prophetic witnesses to testify of the true God with extraordinary power.
- Some believe these witnesses will be Moses and Elijah.
- Others think they will be Enoch and Elijah.
- Still others think they will be two entirely new prophets.
- They will minister for the duration of the first half of the tribulation period.
- The antichrist will then execute them.
- God will resurrect them from the dead, adding credence to everything they professed.

TODAY'S TRANSFORMING TRUTHS

- The two witnesses will be immortal up until God's chosen day for their deaths. The same is true of you and me. We cannot die until God's chosen day for us (Job 14:5; Psalm 139:16). So don't fear death!
- The tribulation period will be the darkest time in human history. And yet God will continue to shine His light during this period through His two mighty prophets and 144,000 Jewish evangelists. Let's follow their lead: "Let your light shine before others, so that they may see your good works and give glory to your Father who is in heaven" (Matthew 5:16).

Day 18

The Seven Seal Judgments
Are Unleashed

The tribulation period will be characterized by the unleashing of God's ever-worsening judgments. That's one reason it is called the "tribulation period." There will be a lot of tribulation.

> The word ***tribulation*** literally means "to press" (as grapes), "to press together," "to press hard upon," and refers to times of oppression, affliction, and distress. The Greek word *thlipsis* is translated variously as "tribulation," "affliction," "anguish," "persecution," "trouble," and "burden."

This word has been used concerning:

1. Those "hard-pressed" by the calamities of war (Matthew 24:21),
2. a woman giving birth to a child (John 16:21),
3. great anxiety and burden of the heart (2 Corinthians 2:4),
4. those "pressed" by poverty and lack (Philippians 4:14),
5. the afflictions of Christ (Colossians 1:24), and
6. a period during the end times that will have unparalleled tribulation (Revelation 7:14).

General tribulation must be distinguished from the tribulation period during the end times. All Christians can expect general tribulation in their lives. Jesus said to the disciples, "In the world you will have tribulation" (John 16:33). Paul and Barnabas also warned that "through many tribulations we must enter the kingdom of God" (Acts 14:22).

The end-time tribulation period is distinct from general tribulation. Prophetic Scripture speaks of a definite period of tribulation at the end of the age (Matthew 24:29-35). It will be of such severity that no period in history—past or future—will equal it (Matthew 24:21). It is called the time of Jacob's trouble, for it is a judgment on Messiah-rejecting Israel (Jeremiah 30:7; Daniel 12:1-4). The nations will also be judged for their sin and rejection of Christ (Isaiah 26:21; Revelation 6:15-17). This period will last seven years, and it will be so bad that people will want to hide and even die (Daniel 9:24, 27; Revelation 6:16).

The book of Revelation reveals that human suffering will steadily escalate during the tribulation period.

The **seal judgments** are the first set of God's wrathful judgments to be unleashed on the earth during the tribulation period.

Consider the horror of these judgments:

First Seal Judgment: The rider of the white horse—the antichrist—goes out to conquer and make war (Revelation 6:1-2).

Second Seal Judgment: Peace is taken from the earth, with people killing each other worldwide (6:3-4).

Third Seal Judgment: Widespread famine emerges, probably due to war breaking out worldwide, causing a disruption in transportation and distribution of food supplies (6:5-6).

Fourth Seal Judgment: Massive casualties result from widespread famine and pestilence, further aggravated by predatory wild beasts (6:7-8).

Fifth Seal Judgment: Massive numbers of God's people are mercilessly martyred (6:9-11).

Sixth Seal Judgment: A devastating earthquake is accompanied by severe cosmic disturbances, with people everywhere trying to hide (6:12-17).

Seventh Seal Judgment: This final seal judgment unleashes a new set of judgments—the trumpet judgments—which are even more catastrophic (see Revelation 8). Things go from bad to worse during the tribulation period.

FAST FACTS ON THE FOUR HORSEMEN OF THE APOCALYPSE

Jesus refers to the **four horsemen of the apocalypse** as a metaphorical way of describing four prophecies that will unfold early on during the tribulation period.

These prophecies of Jesus parallel the prophecies of four of the seal judgments in the book of Revelation. For example, Jesus prophetically speaks of the rise of false christs (Matthew 24:4-5); the first seal judgment involves the rise of the antichrist (Revelation 6:1-2). Jesus prophetically speaks of wars and rumors of wars (Matthew 24:6); the second seal involves the outbreak of war in which nations rise against each other (Revelation 6:3-4). Jesus prophetically speaks of famines (Matthew 24:7); the third seal involves famine (Revelation 6:5-6). Jesus prophetically speaks of earthquakes (Matthew 24:7); the sixth seal involves an earthquake (Revelation 6:12-14).

A comparison of Matthew 24 with Revelation 6 shows that these horrific events occur during the first half of the tribulation period. Woe to those living on earth during this time, for things are about to get even worse.

FAST FACTS ON GOD AS A JUDGE

God is a God of love and mercy, but He is also a God of judgment and wrath. Remember that God judged Adam and Eve, expelling them from the Garden of Eden (Genesis 3). He judged the corrupt world of Noah's day, sending a flood to destroy humankind (Genesis 6–8). He judged Sodom and Gomorrah with a volcanic catastrophe (Genesis 18–19).

God also unleashed upon Egypt the terrors of the ten plagues (Exodus 7–12). He judged those who worshiped the golden calf, using the Levites as His executioners (Exodus 32:26-35). He judged Israel for unfaithfulness to Him after entering Canaan, causing the people to go into captivity (see the book of Daniel).

As well, judgment fell upon the Jews for rejecting Jesus Christ (Matthew 21:43), upon Ananias and Sapphira for lying to God (Acts 5), upon Herod for his self-exalting pride (Acts 12:21), and upon Christians in Corinth who were afflicted with severe illness and even death in response to their irreverence in connection with the Lord's Supper (1 Corinthians 11:29-32; see also 1 John 5:16).

Christians will one day stand before the judgment seat of Christ (1 Corinthians 3:12-15; 2 Corinthians 5:10). Unbelievers will be judged at the great white throne judgment (Revelation 20:11-15).

FREQUENTLY ASKED QUESTIONS

Since Jesus will ride a white horse at the second coming (Revelation 19:11), is it possible that the first horseman of the apocalypse, who rides a white horse, is Jesus and not the antichrist?

I do not think so. The contexts are entirely different. Revelation 19:12 reveals that Christ—wearing "many diadems"—will return to the earth as a conqueror on a horse at the end of the tribulation period. By contrast, Revelation 6 speaks of a rider on a horse at the beginning of the tribulation, in association with three other horses and their riders, all connected to the seal judgments. The rider of the first seal judgment wears a single crown instead of the "many diadems" of Jesus Christ. He is a lesser ruler. Most Bible expositors believe this rider is the antichrist (compare to Daniel 9:26).

What kinds of cosmic disturbances will afflict the earth when the seal judgments are unleashed?

Revelation 6:12 tells us, "When he opened the sixth seal, I looked, and behold, there was a great earthquake, and the sun became black as sackcloth, the full moon became like blood." This massive earthquake may be accompanied by volcanic eruptions that spew voluminous amounts of ash and debris into the atmosphere. This, in turn, causes the sun to darken and the light of the moon to appear red (see Zechariah 14:6-7).

Cosmic phenomena continue with the trumpet judgments: "The fourth angel blew his trumpet, and a third of the sun was struck, and a third of the moon, and a third of the stars, so that a third of their light might be darkened, and a third of the day might be kept from shining, and likewise a third of the night" (Revelation 8:12). Cosmic disturbances will also occur just before the second coming of Christ: "Immediately after the tribulation of those days the sun will be darkened, and the moon will not give its light, and the stars will fall from heaven, and the powers of the heavens will be shaken. Then will appear in heaven the sign of the Son of Man, and then all the tribes of the earth will mourn, and they will see the Son of Man coming on the clouds of heaven with power and great glory" (Matthew 24:29-30; see also Isaiah 13:10). It is hard to imagine the horror!

TODAY'S BIG IDEAS

- Everyone experiences general tribulation throughout life.

- General tribulation is distinct from the future "tribulation period," which will be the worst period of tribulation ever to hit planet Earth.

- The seal judgments will be unleashed during the first half of the tribulation period. There will be bloodshed, famine, death, economic upheaval, a great earthquake, and various cosmic disturbances.

- Four seal judgments parallel Jesus' prophecies of the future in His Olivet Discourse (Matthew 24–25).

- Things will then go from bad to worse with the subsequent unleashing of the trumpet judgments and the bowl judgments.

TODAY'S TRANSFORMING TRUTHS

- The horrors of the tribulation period ought to serve as a motivation for apologetics and evangelism (Matthew 28:19; 1 Peter 3:15; Jude 3). Don't leave these tasks up to pastors and ministers alone. Each of us needs to be involved. Each of us can make a difference. As someone said, "Every pebble—large or small—can make ripples in a pond."

- Don't be fearful. Recognize that God is bringing about His eternal purposes, even when the world seems tumultuous (Deuteronomy 10:14; 1 Chronicles 29:12; 2 Chronicles 20:6; Job 42:2; Psalm 33:8-11; Isaiah 46:10; Ephesians 1:20-22).

Day 19

The Seven Trumpet Judgments Are Unleashed

The seal judgments are bad. The trumpet judgments are worse.

> The **trumpet judgments** are the second set of God's wrathful judgments to be unleashed on the earth during the tribulation period.

So bad are the trumpet judgments that there will be 30 minutes of silence in heaven after heaven's inhabitants become aware of the impending judgments. The book of Revelation documents that God's judgments will escalate dramatically—in both intensity and frequency—throughout the tribulation period.

The first trumpet judgment will entail hail and fire being unleashed upon the earth. This reminds us of one of God's plagues on the Egyptians at the hands of Moses (Exodus 9:18-26). This judgment will cause a catastrophic environmental catastrophe: A third of the earth, a third of the trees, and all the green grass on earth will be "burned up" (Revelation 8:7). Such massive burning may imply that much of the earth's crops will also be destroyed, thus further depleting food supplies on an already-starving planet. These fires may come directly from the hand of God, or possibly from nuclear detonations.

The second trumpet judgment will entail a "fiery mountain" plummeting into the sea, thereby turning it bloody. This "fiery mountain" has been interpreted variously—an enormous mass spewed from a volcano, something that falls from outer space, or perhaps a nuclear missile plunging into the sea and detonating. The waters turning bloody could be the actual blood of dead sea creatures. The death of a third of earth's sea creatures cuts further into the world's food supply, which, in turn, devastates an already-damaged world economy.

The third trumpet judgment will entail a star falling from heaven (Revelation 8:10-11). This "star" may be a case of near-extinction-level impact of a giant meteor or asteroid striking the earth. It appears to be a "star" because it bursts into flames—burning like a torch—as it plummets through the earth's atmosphere. It turns a third of the waters bitter so that people who drink those waters will die. Today's top scientists say that it is not a matter of *if* such a celestial body will strike the earth, it is a matter of *when* it will happen. The mathematical probabilities render this a certainty in the future.

The fourth trumpet judgment will entail severe cosmic disturbances. As Revelation 8:12-13 puts it, "A third of the sun was struck, and a third of the moon, and a third of the stars, so that a third of their light might be darkened, and a third of the day might be kept from shining, and likewise a third of the night." It may well be that the diminishing of light is due to the massive amount of dust kicked up into the atmosphere when the giant meteor or asteroid associated with the third trumpet judgment strikes the earth. All of this will cause a lowering of temperatures globally. Also, with one-third of the trees already being destroyed, there will be much less firewood to keep people warm. With the diminished light, the growth of plant life will be hindered, thereby further reducing the food supply. Things continue to go from bad to worse.

The fifth trumpet judgment will entail hideous demons with scorpion-like power being released from the bottomless pit, after which they engage in relentless torment of human beings for five months (Revelation 9:1-12). Victims of scorpion bites are typically in agony, sometimes succumbing to foaming at the mouth and grinding their teeth in pain. These demonic spirits will inflict torturous wounds that could be physical, spiritual, or both. During this time, people will seek death but be unable to escape their pain. They will long for death rather than repenting before a holy God.

The sixth trumpet judgment will entail fallen angels bound at the Euphrates being released so they can kill a third of humankind by plagues (Revelation 9:13-21). Biblically, a plague is a disease or epidemic caused by or allowed by God for judgment. There will be a massive outbreak of plagues in the end times (see Revelation 6:8; 9:18, 20; 11:6; 15:1, 6, 8; 16:9, 21; 18:4, 8; 21:9; 22:18). Amazingly, those who survive these horrific plagues will "not repent of the works of their hands nor give up worshiping demons and idols of gold and silver and bronze and stone and wood, which cannot see or hear or walk," nor will they "repent of their murders or their sorceries or their sexual immorality or their thefts" (9:20-21). The hearts of human beings will be calloused and hardened against God.

The seventh trumpet judgment will entail unleashing a whole new series of judgments—*the bowl judgments*. These will be worse still than the trumpet judgments (see Revelation 16).

FAST FACTS ON THE CAUSE-EFFECT RELATIONSHIP BETWEEN THE JUDGMENTS

God's judgments often have a cause-effect relationship with each other. In other words, *one judgment is so closely connected to another judgment that it seems like there is a causal relationship.*

In the first seal judgment, the antichrist goes out to make war (Revelation 6:1-2). In the second seal judgment, peace is taken from the earth and people slay each other (Revelation 6:3-4). This illustrates cause and effect. One judgment leads to another.

The third seal judgment involves famine (Revelation 6:5-6). In war (which, in this case, results from the first seal judgment), there is often a disruption in transportation and distribution of supplies—including food supplies. Also, when people slay each other (which results from the second seal judgment), there are fewer people to produce food and distribute it around the world. We again witness cause and effect among these judgments.

The fourth seal judgment involves massive casualties that result from the widespread famine caused by the previous seal judgment (Revelation 6:7-8). Cause and effect!

The meteor striking the earth in the third trumpet judgment (Revelation 8:12-13) likely leads to the fourth trumpet judgment, involving a reduction of light from the sun, moon, and stars as dust is kicked up into the atmosphere after the meteor makes a catastrophic impact.

When studying prophecy, it is often wise to pay attention to cause-and-effect relationships.

FREQUENTLY ASKED QUESTIONS

Is it possible that nuclear weaponry may be used during the tribulation period?

I've alluded to this several times in the book. *Yes, it is possible.* It is hard *not* to suspect the use of nuclear weapons when we read of how much of the earth will be burned up. Further, Revelation 16:2 tells us that people worldwide will break out with loathsome and malignant sores. Could this result be from radiation poisoning following the detonation of nuclear weapons? Some believe Jesus may have been alluding to nuclear weaponry when He spoke of "people fainting with fear and with foreboding of what is coming on the world. *For the powers of the heavens will be shaken*" (Luke 21:26; emphasis added).

Do the trumpet judgments prove the rapture occurs at the midpoint of the tribulation period?

Midtribulationists note that the rapture occurs "at the last trumpet" (1 Corinthians 15:52). Since the "seventh trumpet" sounds in the middle of the tribulation period, they think this must mean that the rapture occurs at that point.

This is faulty reasoning. Theologian Charles Ryrie notes: "This is a somewhat simplistic argument that assumes that all blowing of trumpets must indicate the same kind of event. This is not true. In Jewish apocalyptic literature, trumpets signaled many great eschatological events, including judgments, the gathering of the elect, and resurrection."[17]

We see notable differences when we examine the contexts in which the various eschatological trumpets are sounded. For example, the trumpet in 1 Corinthians 15:52 relates specifically to the rapture and glorification. The same is true of the trumpet mentioned in 1 Thessalonians 4:13-17. However, the trumpet of Revelation 11:15 is unrelated to the rapture, and instead, deals with the unleashing of judgment upon an unbelieving world. Hence, these verses are not supportive of midtribulationism.

TODAY'S BIG IDEAS

- God's judgments during the tribulation period will go from bad to worse.

- They escalate dramatically in both intensity and frequency throughout the tribulation period.

- The trumpet judgments involve hail and fire mixed with blood falling upon the earth, the sea turning to blood, water turning bitter and poisonous, further cosmic disturbances, affliction by demonic scorpions, and the death of a third of humankind.

TODAY'S TRANSFORMING TRUTHS

- Many people during the tribulation period will refuse repentance. However, it is wisest to repent early, as soon as one becomes aware of sin. Early repentance can avert God's judgment. For the Christian, early repentance can avert God's discipline: "If we judged ourselves truly, we would not be judged" (1 Corinthians 11:31).

- The apostle Paul urged, "Do not be conformed to this world, but be transformed by the renewal of your mind" (Romans 12:2). The world system is headed for God's judgment. "Do you not know that friendship with the world is enmity with God?" (James 4:4). Let's keep our priorities straight.

- People during the tribulation period will have no fear of God. You and I know it is wise to live in reverent fear of God (1 Samuel 12:14, 24; 2 Chronicles 19:9; Acts 10:35; 1 Peter 1:17; 2:17). Fear of God motivates obedience (Deuteronomy 5:29; Ecclesiastes 12:13), encourages the avoidance of evil (Proverbs 3:7; 8:13; 16:6), and brings God's blessing (Psalm 115:13).

Day 20

The Rise of
Religious New Babylon

Babylon will rise again. It is described in Revelation 17–18 and is best dubbed "New Babylon."

New Babylon plays two different roles during the first and second halves of the tribulation period respectively. *Religious New Babylon*—dominant during the first half of the tribulation period—is described in Revelation 17. *Political and commercial New Babylon*—in power during the second half of the tribulation period—is described in chapter 18.

> **Religious New Babylon** is called a "great prostitute," referring to this religion's unfaithfulness to God, idolatry, and apostasy (Jeremiah 3:6-9; Ezekiel 20:30; Hosea 4:15; 5:3; 6:10; 9:1). During the first half of the tribulation period, this false religion will influence the people in nations all around the earth (Revelation 17:1).

Revelation 17:9 speaks of the "seven mountains on which the woman [the prostitute] is seated" (insert added for clarity). The seven mountains symbolize seven kingdoms and their kings (verse 10). Mountains often symbolize kingdoms in Scripture (Psalm 30:7; Jeremiah 51:25; Daniel 2:44-45). These seven kingdoms are the seven great world empires—Egypt, Assyria, Babylon, Medo-Persia, Greece, Rome, and the future kingdom of the antichrist.

The biblical text tells us that five kingdoms have fallen, one still exists, and one is yet to come (Revelation 17:10). At the time of John's writing, the Egyptian, Assyrian, Babylonian, Medo-Persian, and Greek empires had already fallen. Rome still existed at the time of John's writing. The antichrist's kingdom is yet future. False paganized religion has affected—or will affect—all these empires. That is what is meant by the woman who was seated upon the seven mountains (or kingdoms).

This apostate religious system will exercise powerful political clout (verses 12-13). It will seem outwardly glorious while being inwardly corrupt (verse 4). It will persecute all true believers (verse 6).

This false religion will even control the antichrist for a time: The great "prostitute"—the false religious system—will *sit on* (and thus control) "a scarlet beast," who is the antichrist (Revelation 17:3). There is initially a close connection between the false religious system and the antichrist because both are unfaithful to God and are idolatrous.

However, the antichrist—along with ten kings under his authority—will eventually destroy the false world religion (Revelation 17:16-18). This will likely take place at the midpoint of the tribulation period. The antichrist will come into both global political dominion *and* religious dominion—demanding even to be worshiped as god (Daniel 11:36-38; 2 Thessalonians 2:4; Revelation 13:8, 15).

To clarify, the antichrist will destroy only the religion, not the city of New Babylon. At the midpoint of the tribulation period, New Babylon will transition into the economic and political center of the world.

FAST FACTS ON BABYLON IN REVELATION

The book of Revelation contains 404 verses. Out of those, 44 deal with Babylon. This means that more than 10 percent of Revelation deals with Babylon.

While Jerusalem is God's city in the Bible (Revelation 21:2-3), Babylon is a demonic city (18:2). Revelation describes the New Jerusalem as a chaste bride (21:9-10) and New Babylon as a great prostitute (17:1, 3). The New Jerusalem is an eternal city (Revelation 21:1-4), while New Babylon is a temporal city that God will destroy (18:8).

New Babylon is explicitly identified as a "great city" (17:18) and will have global importance (17:15, 18). It will be closely connected with the antichrist (17:3). The city will be a bastion of false religion during the first half of the tribulation period (17:4-5; 18:1-2). The city will eventually become a global commerce center during the second half of the tribulation (18:9-19). New Babylon will persecute God's people (17:6; 18:20, 24).

FAST FACTS ON A LITERAL NEW BABYLON DURING THE END TIMES

New Babylon will be a literal city during the tribulation period. We can say this with strong confidence because other geographical locations in the book of Revelation are literal—such as the cities of the seven churches in Revelation 2 and 3.

The only time in Revelation where a city is not literal is where Revelation explicitly tells us it is not literal. Revelation 11:8 refers to Jerusalem as "the great city that symbolically is called Sodom and Egypt." This implies that all other geographical references in Revelation are literal.

New Babylon is mentioned in the same context as the Euphrates River, showing that a literal city is meant (Revelation 9:14 and 16:12). There is also a close connection between the book of Revelation and the book of Daniel. In Daniel, Babylon is *without exception* a literal city. Revelation 17–18 likewise draws heavily from Jeremiah 50–51. Because Jeremiah was undeniably speaking of a literal Babylon, we can conclude that John was speaking of a literal Babylon in Revelation.

FREQUENTLY ASKED QUESTIONS

Is it possible that religious New Babylon in Revelation 17—the "great prostitute"—is the Roman Catholic Church?

Many today believe so. This view became popular during the Reformation period. This theory is built on the harlot motif (Revelation 17:1). Just as a harlot is sexually unfaithful, it is alleged the Roman Catholic Church has long been unfaithful to God. Proponents of this view also note how the great prostitute is adorned: "The woman was arrayed in purple and scarlet, and adorned with gold and jewels and pearls" (Revelation 17:4). This seems similar to the colors of papal and cardinal robes.

While such a view is possible, a notable problem is that many of those who hold to the view that the harlot is Roman Catholicism also hold to the belief that the beast of Revelation is Roman Catholicism. This is problematic since the harlot and the beast are portrayed in Revelation as distinct from one another. By the end of Revelation 17, the beast is portrayed as destroying the harlot.

Critics also suggest that commentators who hold to this view are reading their own current historical experiences into the text of Scripture. This view emerged during the time of the Reformation, when men like John Calvin and Martin Luther took hard stands against Roman Catholicism. It is easy to see how Roman Catholicism could be "read into" the harlot or beast of Revelation.

Finally, one must wonder how a theory involving an ecclesiastical institution centuries after Revelation was written could have had any immediate relevance to the original readers of the book of Revelation. Would they have understood the text in this way? Many expositors think not.

Is it possible that religious New Babylon is apostate Christendom?

It is possible. This theory, too, relies heavily on the harlot motif (Revelation 17:1). Just as a harlot is sexually unfaithful, so apostate Christianity is unfaithful to God and true Christianity. Some describe it in terms of adultery. Adultery implies that at one time there was faithfulness, but since its original faithfulness, there has been infidelity. In this theory, many of those left behind after the rapture will be a part of this apostate Christianity.

A problem with this view involves the question of relevance to the original readers of Revelation. Would they have understood it this way? It is unlikely.

Might religious New Babylon be some general and broad form of paganism?

It's possible. The "prostitute" (or false religion) is said to be seated on "seven mountains"—a metaphorical reference to seven kingdoms: Egypt, Assyria, Babylon, Medo-Persia, Greece, Rome, and that of the antichrist. Five of the kingdoms have fallen, one still exists, and one is yet to come (Revelation 17:10). Whatever this false religion is, it has affected (or will affect) all these empires. Paganism has historically been on religious center stage in Egypt, Assyria, Babylon, Medo-Persia, Greece, and Rome. Therefore, it is reasonable to assume that some form of paganism will be central to the false religion of New Babylon.

What is your assessment?

Perhaps the false religion will be a hybrid religion—*a religious amalgamation*—that mixes Roman Catholicism, Eastern Orthodoxy, Liberal Protestantism, and paganism. These may converge into an ecclesiastical New Babylon.

TODAY'S BIG IDEAS

- Babylon will rise again—New Babylon.

- New Babylon will be a literal city—first acting as a head-quarters for a global false religion and then as a political and commercial center for the antichrist.

- The false religion will probably be a hybrid religion—a religious amalgamation.

- The antichrist will destroy the false religion at the midpoint of the tribulation period. He will be the sole object of worship on earth from then forward.

TODAY'S TRANSFORMING TRUTHS

- Religious New Babylon will be responsible for the deaths of many believers during the tribulation period (Revelation 17:6). Here is a question to ponder: *Would you be willing to die in defending the truth about Jesus Christ?*

- The religious landscape is now peppered with cults, false religions, and other false worldviews. These set the stage for the eventual emergence of a global false religion associated with New Babylon. Here is a challenge: Let us seek to reach those engulfed in deception (Matthew 28:19). Get involved in apologetics (1 Peter 3:15; Jude 3). I recommend *The Comprehensive Guide to Apologetics*, edited by Joseph Holden (Harvest House Publishers).

Day 21

The Antichrist's Wound and Apparent Resurrection

We now find ourselves at the midpoint of the tribulation period. The antichrist will now catapult himself into absolute political and religious dominion on planet Earth. To accomplish this, he will need to do away with anyone or anything that stands in his way—especially in the religious realm. He will destroy religious New Babylon, execute God's two prophetic witnesses, break his covenant with Israel, put an end to the Jewish sacrificial system of worship, and then enthrone himself within the Jewish temple.

First, however, he needs to do something spectacular...*something that will rouse the world to worship him*. He needs to die and resurrect from the dead—or at least convince the world that he has come back from the dead, whether or not he has really done so.

Bible interpreters debate whether the antichrist will truly resurrect from the dead. Some prophecy scholars say it will be a bogus resurrection. Others say it will be genuine. Let's briefly consider each view:

1. Some prophecy scholars believe the antichrist will suffer a head wound that is most often lethal, but in this case is healed by Satan so that the antichrist does not die but lives on. In keeping with this is the biblical affirmation that the antichrist "*seemed* to have a mortal wound" (Revelation 13:3; emphasis added), or "*appeared* to be fatally wounded" (CSB; emphasis added), or it was "*as if* it had been fatally wounded" (NASB; emphasis added). Perhaps the antichrist will *seem to* or *appear to* be killed when he really will not. Perhaps Satan will perform a "Grade-B" miracle in healing him, making it appear to the world that he has resurrected from the dead.

2. Other prophecy scholars believe the antichrist will suffer a mortal head wound that will genuinely kill him, and Satan will resurrect him from the dead. Tim LaHaye and Jerry Jenkins represent this viewpoint: "We believe that the Beast really is killed, for John twice says that he 'ascends out of the bottomless pit' (11:7; 17:8); we believe this means that the Beast is killed, descends to the pit, and ascends from there to the earth when he is resurrected."[18] This is a common view held today.

One problem with this view is that only God is infinite in power (omnipotent); the devil is finite and limited. Only God can create life (Genesis 1:1, 21; Deuteronomy 32:39); the devil cannot (Exodus 8:19). Only God can truly raise the dead (John 10:18; Revelation 1:18). Further, this view doesn't reflect the biblical teaching that the antichrist merely seemed to or appeared to have been killed.

Regardless of which view is correct, the biblical text reveals that people during the tribulation period will *believe* he has been resurrected. People from around the globe will worship him because of it.

If the antichrist does not die, how can we explain his emergence from the abyss? Bible scholar Walter Price offers a viable explanation:

> The apostle Paul...was stoned in Lystra, and the citizens "dragged him out of the city, supposing that he was dead" (Acts 14:19). While in an unconscious state, Paul "was caught up into Paradise, and heard unspeakable words, which it is not lawful for a man to utter" (2 Cor. 12:4). Paul had received what seemed like a death stroke. While he was thought to be dead, his spirit was caught up into the third heaven and there received a profound revelation from God. This same thing, in reverse, will happen to the antichrist. The antichrist...will be no more dead than was the apostle Paul. But just as the citizens of Lystra thought Paul was dead, so the antichrist will be thought dead.[19]

Price raises the possibility that just as Paul's spirit departed from his body and was taken up to God's domain where he received further revelations, so the antichrist's spirit may depart from his body (appearing to be dead) and be taken into the abyss, where Satan will offer the world's kingdoms to him.

> Just as Satan took Jesus up into a high mountain and showed him all the kingdoms of the world, and offered them to him, if he would fall down and worship him; so Satan will take the antichrist into the depths of the Abyss and show him all the kingdoms of the world...Jesus refused to bow down to Satan. The antichrist will not refuse.[20]

Price suggests that the antichrist's spirit will then come forth from the abyss (Revelation 11:7), reenter what appears to be a dead body—giving the appearance of a resurrection from the dead—and continue on his satanically inspired mission. Prophecy expert Mark Hitchcock suggests that while in the abyss, the "Antichrist probably receives his orders and strategy from Satan, literally selling his soul to the devil, and then comes back to earth with hellish ferocity to establish his world domination over a completely awestruck earth."[21]

FAST FACTS ON SATAN'S LIMITATIONS

There is a gigantic difference between Satan and God. Satan does not possess divine attributes that belong to God alone, such as omnipresence (being everywhere-present), omnipotence (being all-powerful), and omniscience (being all-knowing). Satan is a creature, and as a creature, he is lesser than the Creator. He has creaturely limitations.

For example, Satan can only be in one place at a time. His strength, though significant, is limited. And his knowledge, though great, is limited. Only God can create life (Genesis 1:1, 21; Deuteronomy 32:39); the devil cannot (see Exodus 8:19). Only God can truly raise the dead (John 10:18; Revelation 1:18).

One must wonder: If the devil has the power to resurrect people from the dead, why didn't he resurrect dead Roman emperors who were so effective in killing Christians? And why hasn't he resurrected the founders of the various cults and false religions to give them credence? If the devil *could* do so, he *would* do so.

FREQUENTLY ASKED QUESTIONS

What is the difference between God's miracles and Satan's lying wonders, which the latter empowers the antichrist to do (2 Thessalonians 2:9-11)?

> ➲ Some theologians say Satan can do what we might call **Grade-B miracles**.
> ➲ Only God can do heavy-duty **Grade-A miracles**.

Only God can fully control and supersede the natural laws He created. Though on one occasion, He did grant Satan the power to bring a whirlwind on Job's family (Job 1:19). As the account of Job illustrates, all the power the devil has is granted to him by God and is carefully limited and monitored (see Job 1:10-12). Satan is "on a leash." Satan's finite power is under the control of God's infinite power.

Given the scriptural evidence, it seems reasonable to conclude that Satan will either engage in a limited Grade-B miracle in healing the wounded antichrist (that is, *injured* but not *dead*), or he will engage in some kind of masterful deception as the "father of lies" (John 8:44)— or perhaps a combination of both. The world will be amazed and will worship the antichrist as a result.

Why do theologians say Satan is a master counterfeiter?

> Augustine said **Satan is the ape of God**. He "copycats" God in many ways.

Satan has his own church—the "synagogue of Satan" (Revelation 2:9). He has his own ministers—ministers of darkness that bring false sermons (2 Corinthians 11:4-5). He has formulated his own system of theology—called "teachings of demons" (1 Timothy 4:1; see also

Revelation 2:24). His ministers proclaim a counterfeit gospel—"a gospel contrary to the one we preached to you" (Galatians 1:7-8).

Satan has his own throne (Revelation 13:2) and his own worshipers (13:4). He inspires false christs and self-constituted messiahs (Matthew 24:4-5). He employs false teachers who bring in "destructive heresies" (2 Peter 2:1). He sends out false prophets (Matthew 24:11) and sponsors false apostles who imitate the true ones (2 Corinthians 11:13).

As related to the antichrist, a resurrection—or what *appears* to be a resurrection—would be in perfect keeping with Satan's deceptive character as a copycat.

TODAY'S BIG IDEAS

- Christian Bible interpreters differ over whether the antichrist will be resurrected during the tribulation period.

- Some believe the antichrist will suffer a head wound that is usually lethal, but in this case is healed by Satan, so that the antichrist does not die but lives on.

- Others believe the antichrist will suffer a mortal head wound that will kill him, and Satan will resurrect him from the dead.

- In any event, the world's people will *believe* the antichrist has been resurrected from the dead and will worship him as god.

TODAY'S TRANSFORMING TRUTHS

- I urge you to test all experiences against the Word of God (Acts 17:11; 1 Thessalonians 5:21). After all, the mere witnessing of something apparently supernatural does not necessarily point to the truth. Just as people can be deceived by savvy Las Vegas magicians, so people can be deceived by bogus miracles. These are days for discernment.

- It is wise for us to daily feast on God's Word so we can fortify our minds with God's wisdom, enabling us to discern and stand against satanic deceptions (Psalm 119:105; 2 Timothy 3:15-17).

Day 22

Upheavals at the Midpoint of the Tribulation

Several "shakeups" occur in heaven and on earth at the midpoint of the tribulation period. Here we will briefly address three of them: Satan's ousting from heaven, the destruction of religious New Babylon, and the execution of God's two prophetic witnesses.

SATAN'S OUSTING FROM HEAVEN

Satan—"the accuser of our brothers"—will be once and for all ousted from heaven at the midpoint of the tribulation period (Revelation 12:10, 12-13). There are opposite responses to this ousting—*rejoicing* in heaven and *woe* for those on earth (verse 12). There is rejoicing in heaven because Satan will no longer have direct access before God to engage in his role as "accuser of our brothers" (verse 10).

Woe comes upon those still on earth, for Satan will be filled with fury, knowing his time is short. Since only half the tribulation period remains, he knows he now has a mere 1,260 days before meeting his doom. Things will go from bad to worse for the inhabitants of the earth, for Satan "now moves among them more antagonistically than ever."[22]

RELIGIOUS NEW BABYLON WILL BE DESTROYED

With the assistance of ten kings under his authority, the antichrist will destroy religious New Babylon—the religious "prostitute" of the end times (Revelation 17:16). There are no textual indicators or clues in the book of Revelation as to the precise timing of this event. However, it seems most logical and coherent to place it midpoint during the tribulation period, at the same time that the antichrist assumes the role of a world dictator by proclamation (Daniel 9:27; Matthew 24:15). The antichrist will come into both political dominion *and* religious dominion globally, demanding worship as God by those on earth (Daniel 11:36-38; 2 Thessalonians 2:4; Revelation 13:8, 15). To facilitate worship by all of earth's inhabitants, the antichrist will first need to dispose of this world religion. He alone will now occupy the religious center stage. No competing religious system will be permitted.

GOD'S TWO PROPHETIC WITNESSES ARE EXECUTED AND RESURRECTED

God will raise up two mighty prophetic witnesses who will testify to the true God with incredible power. They will perform miracles reminiscent of Elijah (1 Kings 17; Malachi 4:5) and Moses (Exodus 7–11). They will emerge on the scene at the beginning of the tribulation period and minister for three-and-a-half years (Revelation 11:3).

At the midpoint of the tribulation period, the antichrist will execute the two witnesses. Revelation 11:8-12 provides the details of this execution and its aftermath:

1. The bodies of the witnesses will lie lifeless in Jerusalem (metaphorically called "Sodom and Egypt"). People worldwide will gaze at their bodies for three days— apparently via television and online. Remember, the refusal to bury a corpse was, during Bible times, a way of showing contempt (Deuteronomy 21:22-23; Acts 14:19).

2. The people of the world will have a "Christmas" celebration upon the execution of these two witnesses. They will exchange presents, apparently in relief that the prophets are no longer around.

3. God will then turn the tables: "A breath of life from God entered them, and they stood up on their feet, and great fear fell on those who saw them." Christmas-like celebrations will quickly give way to fear as people witness this mighty

act of God. The resurrection and ascension of the two witnesses will serve as an epic conclusion and testimony to the prophetic words they spoke during their ministry.

FAST FACTS ON SATAN'S JUDGMENTS

There are five other judgments of Satan, aside from the one that leads to his ousting from heaven at the midpoint of the tribulation period (Revelation 12:9). Satan was cast from his original position of privilege in heaven following his fall (Ezekiel 28:16). He was judged in the garden of Eden (Genesis 3:14-15). He was judged at the cross (John 12:31; Colossians 2:15; Hebrews 2:14). He will be confined in the abyss during the millennial kingdom (Revelation 20:2). He will be cast into the lake of fire after the millennial kingdom (Revelation 20:10; see Matthew 25:41).

FAST FACTS ON GOD'S "BREATH"

At creation, "God formed the man of dust from the ground and breathed into his nostrils the breath of life, and the man became a living creature" (Genesis 2:7).

God's breath also brought Israel back from the dead. According to the prophecy of the dry bones, God's breath, during the end times, would enter Israel, after which Israel would come to life again (Ezekiel 37:5). This was fulfilled at the rebirth of the nation of Israel in 1948.

In terms of the two prophetic witnesses, "a breath of life from God" will enter them (Revelation 11:11). They will resurrect from the dead and ascend into heaven.

God is a master of bringing new life!

FAST FACTS ON THE COMMAND "COME UP HERE!"

The apostle John was commanded to "come up here" in Revelation 4:1, to receive God's great prophetic revelation of the future. The two prophetic witnesses, after being resurrected from the dead, "heard a loud voice from heaven saying to them, 'Come up here!' And they went up to heaven in a cloud" (Revelation 11:12). The rapture will occur with a "cry of command" (1 Thessalonians 4:16). One wonders if the cry of command will be "Come up here!"

FREQUENTLY ASKED QUESTIONS

How is Satan an "accuser of the brothers"?

Accusing God's people is Satan's ongoing work—he does it "day and night" (Revelation 12:10). He accuses God's people in two ways. First, he accuses believers before the throne of God (Job 1:6; 2:1; Zechariah 3:1; Romans 8:33). Second, he accuses believers to their own consciences, seeking to inflict excessive guilt in order to bring on depression and feelings of defeat.

Of course, no accusation of Satan against any believer in Jesus can stand because their sins have been forgiven based upon the shed blood of the Lamb (Romans 8:33-39). In the end, Satan's accusations against believers are fruitless.

Why does God let the two prophetic witnesses die?

Once the two prophetic witnesses have completed their work of ministry, God will sovereignly permit the beast (the antichrist) to kill them. Notice that the biblical text reveals they will be executed "when they have finished their testimony" (Revelation 11:7). The word "finished" in this verse is the same word used by Jesus upon the cross when He said, "It is finished" (John 19:30). Christ died after He had finished His work of redemption. The two witnesses will die after they complete their work of redemptive ministry.

Let us not forget that God is in charge of when all human beings die. God has allotted a specific time on earth for each of us. As Job said to God, a person's "days are determined, and the number of his months is with you, and you have appointed his limits that he cannot pass" (Job 14:5).

In a similar manner, the apostle Paul said that God "himself gives to all mankind life and breath and everything. And he made from one man every nation of mankind to live on all the face of the earth, having determined allotted periods and the boundaries of their dwelling place" (Acts 17:25-26). Paul's words about God "having determined allotted periods" reflects the words of the psalmist: "In your book were written, every one of them, the days that were formed for me, when as yet there was none of them" (Psalm 139:16).

Why is Jerusalem figuratively called "Sodom and Egypt" in Revelation 11:8?

During the second half of the tribulation period, Jerusalem—especially after the city becomes dominated by the antichrist, with his throne in the Jewish temple—will become an anti-God city. Sodom was a city brimming with perversion and rebellion, while Egypt was known for its persecution of God's people. Both places were viewed as rebellious against God. The description of Jerusalem as "Sodom and Egypt" shows that this once-holy city will, during the second half of the tribulation period, be vile and corrupt.

TODAY'S BIG IDEAS

- Satan will be ousted from heaven at the midpoint of the tribulation period. This brings rejoicing to the inhabitants of heaven, but woe to the earth's inhabitants.

- Religious New Babylon will be destroyed at the midpoint of the tribulation. The antichrist alone will now take center stage in the religious world.

- The antichrist will execute God's two prophetic witnesses at the midpoint of the tribulation. While earth's inhabitants initially celebrate their demise, they soon succumb to dread when the two witnesses resurrect from the dead and ascend into heaven.

TODAY'S TRANSFORMING TRUTHS

- While Satan is the "accuser of our brothers" who seeks to condemn Christians (Revelation 12:10), Romans 8:1 promises, "There is therefore now no condemnation for those who are in Christ Jesus." *No condemnation whatsoever!* We are forgiven through the blood of the Lamb (Romans 8:33-39). Satan is defeated! Rejoice in this.

- The antichrist will be permitted to execute God's two witnesses only "when they have finished their testimony" (Revelation 11:7). We learn from this that we cannot die until our work on earth is done. Until that day, stay busy for the Lord. "Whatever you do, work heartily, as for the Lord and not for men, knowing that from the Lord you will receive the inheritance as your reward" (Colossians 3:23-24).

Day 23

The Antichrist Desolates the Jewish Temple

The covenant the antichrist will sign with Israel is intended to remain in effect for the entire seventieth week of Daniel—the duration of the tribulation period. But the antichrist will double-cross Israel: "For half of the week he shall put an end to sacrifice and offering" (Daniel 9:27). This means that after the covenant has been in effect for three-and-a-half years, the antichrist will renege on the covenant and cause Israel's temple sacrifices to cease.

The antichrist will have already relocated from the revived Roman Empire to the land of Israel: "He shall pitch his palatial tents between the sea and the glorious holy mountain" (Daniel 11:45). It thus appears that the antichrist will invade the holy land at the midpoint of the tribulation period and then prohibit further sacrifices in the Jewish temple.

Why cause the sacrifices to cease? The antichrist—having already attained global political power—will now seek to assume global dominion over the religious realm as well. This sets the context for the abomination of desolation.

Jesus Himself prophesied the desecration of the future Jewish temple: "The day is coming when you will see what Daniel the prophet spoke about—the sacrilegious object that causes desecration standing in the Holy Place" (Matthew 24:15 NLT). Jesus was referring to Daniel 11:31, where the prophet Daniel said that the antichrist's army "will take over the Temple fortress, pollute the sanctuary, put a stop to the daily sacrifices, and set up the sacrilegious object that causes desecration" (NLT).

The antichrist—the "man of lawlessness" (2 Thessalonians 2:3-4)—will not only sit within the Jewish temple, but will also set up an image of himself inside (Daniel 9:27; Matthew 24:15). This will be an abomination to the Jews.

> The word ***abomination*** comes from a root term that means "to make foul" or "stink." It refers to something that makes one feel nauseous, and, by implication, something morally abhorrent and detestable.

The antichrist's sacrilegious act will amount to enthroning himself in the place of deity, displaying himself as God (compare with Isaiah 14:13-14 and Ezekiel 28:2-9). This blasphemous act will desecrate the temple, making it abominable, and therefore desolate. The antichrist—the world dictator—will then demand that the world worship and pay idolatrous homage to him alone. Any who refuse will be persecuted and even martyred.

The fact that the antichrist will "put a stop to the daily sacrifices" in the Jewish temple (Daniel 11:31 NLT) indicates his grotesque self-exaltation. He will not allow competing systems of worship to exist. No one is to be worshiped *but him alone* from that point onward.

The antichrist's claim to be God is in line with the fact that he will be energized by Satan (2 Thessalonians 2:9), who himself had earlier sought godhood (Isaiah 14:13-14; Ezekiel 28:2-9). The antichrist will take on the character of the one who energizes him. As Bible expositor Renald Showers put it, by the middle of the seventieth week, the antichrist "will turn against every form of established worship to clear the way for the worship of himself. He will magnify himself to the level of deity."[23]

There is one further observation to make here. Recall that during His three-year ministry, Jesus cleansed the temple (Mark 11:15-19). By contrast, the antichrist will defile the temple when he sits "in the temple of God, proclaiming himself to be God" (2 Thessalonians 2:4). Truly, the antichrist will be a detestable antithesis of the true Christ.

We may sum up the antichrist's activities related to Israel this way:

➲ While the antichrist was once **Israel's protector**, he now becomes **Israel's persecutor**.

➲ While the antichrist was once **Israel's defender**, he now becomes **Israel's defiler**.

Scripture reveals that things worsen once the abomination of desolation occurs at the midpoint of the tribulation period. Indeed, the events of the second half of the tribulation period are appropriately called "the great tribulation" (Revelation 3:14). As Matthew 24:21 puts it, "There will be great tribulation, such as has not been from the beginning of the world until now, no, and never will be." Daniel 12:1 likewise prophesies: "There shall be a time of trouble, such as never has been since there was a nation till that time." Since this period largely deals with Israel, Jeremiah 30:7 calls it "a time of distress for Jacob" (Jacob representing Israel).

This means that things will become unimaginably traumatic for the Jewish people in Jerusalem at the midpoint of the tribulation period. The antichrist will not only assume global political power but will also declare himself to be God and exalt himself within the Jewish temple. To make matters worse, the antichrist will be afire with passion in persecuting the Jewish people.

FAST FACTS ON ANTIOCHUS EPIPHANES AS A "TYPE" OF THE ANTICHRIST

A *type* may be defined as a figure or representation of something to come. It is an Old Testament institution, event, person, object, or ceremony that has reality and purpose during biblical history, but which also—by God's design— foreshadows something yet to be revealed. Types are therefore prophetic.

Antiochus Epiphanes (215–164 BC) ruled the Seleucid Empire from 175 BC until he died in 164 BC. He was vile, vengeful, and cruel. Biblical interpreters believe Antiochus Epiphanes was a type of the antichrist. Both persecute the Jewish people, even seeking to exterminate them. Both are self-exalting and demand worship. Both defile the Jewish temple, thereby causing an abomination of desolation. (Antiochus Epiphanes sacrificed a pig—an unclean animal—upon the altar of burnt offering in the temple. The antichrist will set up an image of himself in the temple.) A religious leader assists both—the priest Menelaus assisted Antiochus Epiphanes; the false prophet will assist the antichrist.

FREQUENTLY ASKED QUESTIONS

How can we be sure Jesus was not referring to Herod's temple being desecrated during New Testament times?

Jesus was not saying that the abomination of desolation would take place in the Jewish temple of His day. After all, Jesus had already positively affirmed that the great temple built by Herod would be annihilated: "Do you see all these buildings? I tell you the truth, they will be completely demolished. Not one stone will be left on top of another!" (Matthew 24:2 NLT). This prophecy was fulfilled in AD 70 when Titus and his Roman warriors overran Jerusalem and the Jewish temple.

The only conclusion we can reach is that though the temple of Jesus' day would be destroyed, the abomination of desolation would occur in a yet-future temple (Matthew 24:15). This latter temple would be built by the midpoint of the tribulation period (Daniel 9:27; 12:11).

How is the abomination of desolation an act of blasphemy?

The root meaning of the Greek word translated *blasphemy* can range from showing a lack of reverence for God to a more extreme attitude of contempt for either God or something considered sacred (Leviticus 24:16; Matthew 26:65; Mark 2:7). It can involve speaking evil against

God (Psalm 74:18; Isaiah 52:5; Romans 2:24; Revelation 13:1, 6; 16:9, 11, 21). It can also involve showing contempt for the true God by making claims of divinity for oneself (Mark 14:64; John 10:33). The antichrist will engage in all these aspects of blasphemy.

When the antichrist first comes into power, he will appear to be a dynamic, charismatic leader who can solve the world's problems. However, he will deify himself at the midpoint of the tribulation period. He will set up an image of himself in the Jewish temple, thereby desolating it (Matthew 24:15).

Daniel 11:36 confirms that the antichrist "shall exalt himself and magnify himself above every god." We also read in 2 Thessalonians 2:4 that the antichrist ultimately "opposes and exalts himself against every so-called god or object of worship, so that he takes his seat in the temple of God, proclaiming himself to be God." There is no greater blasphemy than this. The antichrist truly is *anti*-Christ, defying the true Christ and putting himself in Christ's place (Revelation 13:5-6).

TODAY'S BIG IDEAS

- The antichrist will set up an image of himself inside the Jewish temple at the midpoint of the tribulation period. This amounts to enthroning himself in the place of deity, displaying himself as God.
- This act of desolation will be an abomination to the Jewish people.
- The antichrist's claim to deity is in line with the fact that he will be energized by Satan (2 Thessalonians 2:9), who himself earlier sought godhood (Isaiah 14:13-14; Ezekiel 28:2-9).
- The antichrist's prohibition of further Jewish sacrifices is motivated by the antichrist's goal of becoming the sole object of worship on earth.
- The antichrist is truly *anti*-Christ. Whereas Jesus *cleansed* the temple, the antichrist will *defile* it.

TODAY'S TRANSFORMING TRUTHS

- Today's lesson highlights the hideousness of self-exaltation. God desires us to walk on the path of humility (Proverbs 27:2; Philippians 2:3; Colossians 3:12; James 4:6, 10). Our lives should exalt Christ and Him alone (John 3:30).
- Christians are the "temple of the Holy Spirit" (1 Corinthians 3:16; 6:19). Let us daily resolve not to defile or desolate this temple by sin.

Day 24

The False Prophet
Exalts the Antichrist

The apostle John introduces us to the false prophet in Revelation 13:11 with the words, "I saw *another* beast" (emphasis added). Just as the antichrist will be a beast, so will the false prophet. The Greek word for "another" is *allos*, meaning "another of the same kind." Together, this beastly duo will wreak havoc upon the earth for seven years.

> ⊃ **False prophets** will sprinkle the religious landscape during the end times (Matthew 24:24). Such prophets will be mouthpieces of Satan, spreading doctrines of demons (1 Timothy 4:1).
>
> ⊃ **A supreme false prophet** will emerge during the tribulation period who will be the antichrist's right-hand man— his "first lieutenant" (Revelation 13:11-18). While the antichrist will primarily be a military and political leader, the false prophet will primarily be a religious leader.

The false prophet will have "two horns like a lamb" (Revelation 13:11). The antichrist will have "ten horns" (13:1). Since horns metaphorically indicate power and authority, we can infer that the false prophet will have less power and authority than the antichrist.

The false prophet will speak "like a dragon" (verse 11). This may mean that he speaks words inspired by the dragon, who is Satan. Just as the Holy Spirit inspires true prophets, so Satan (the *unholy* spirit) will inspire the false prophet. Prophecy expert Ed Hindson says the false prophet "looks religious, but he talks like the devil."[24]

Though the false prophet will have less power than the antichrist, he nevertheless "exercises all the authority of the first beast in its presence" (verse 12). This shows that the authority of the false prophet is a *delegated* authority—that is, he speaks on behalf of the antichrist. Revelation 13:13-15 tells us that the false prophet

> performs great signs, even making fire come down from heaven to earth in front of people, and by the signs that it is allowed to work in the presence of the beast it deceives those who dwell on earth, telling them to make an image for the beast...And it was allowed to give breath to the image of the beast, so that the image of the beast might even speak and might cause those who would not worship the image of the beast to be slain.

One of the false prophet's miraculous acts involves animating an image of the beast in the Jewish temple. The apostle Paul earlier revealed that the antichrist will sit in God's temple (2 Thessalonians 2:4) and receive the worship that properly belongs only to God. When the antichrist is not physically present in the temple, an image of him will be placed there to provide an object of worship in his absence (Revelation 13:14-15; 14:9, 11; 15:2; 16:2; 19:20; 20:4).

The false prophet "gives breath" to the image of the beast so that it can "speak." Whether this is a mechanical deception or a supernatural act, the false prophet is able to give the image the appearance of *being alive.*

The appearance of being alive sets the image of the beast apart from the typical idols from Old Testament times. Psalm 135:15-16 tells us, "The idols of the nations are silver and gold, the work of human hands. They have mouths, but do not speak; they have eyes, but do not see." Likewise, Habakkuk 2:19 warns, "Woe to him who says to a wooden thing, Awake; to a silent stone, Arise! Can this teach? Behold, it is overlaid with gold and silver, and there is no breath at all in it." Contrary to such dead idols, the idolatrous image of the antichrist will seem to be alive, even godlike.

The goal of these supernatural acts will be to induce people worldwide to worship the antichrist. The antichrist will seek the same worship rendered to Christ when He was on earth (see Exodus 34:14).

FAST FACTS ON "SIGNS"

The Greek word for "**sign**" is *semeion* and carries the idea of a miracle that attests to something.

Jesus' signs (miracles) attested that He was who He claimed to be (John 2:11; 4:54; 6:2; 12:18). The apostles' signs (miracles) attested that they were genuine messengers of God (Hebrews 2:3-4). The unspoken assumption is, *Where miracles are, there God is.*

The false prophet's signs are highly deceptive. They seem to support the antichrist's claim to deity. However, these are "false signs and wonders" (2 Thessalonians 2:9).

FAST FACTS ON CHRISTIANS SUCCUMBING TO DECEPTION

Revelation 13:14 says that those who dwell upon the earth will be deceived. Scripture affirms that even God's people can be deceived. For example, Ezekiel 34:1-7 tells us that God's sheep can be led astray by wicked shepherds. Jesus warned His followers to *beware* of false prophets who may appear to be good on the outside but on the inside are very dangerous (Matthew 7:15-16). Jesus warned them because He knew they could be deceived.

The apostle Paul likewise warned Christians against being "led astray from a sincere and pure devotion to Christ" (2 Corinthians 11:3). He also warned the church elders at Ephesus about "fierce wolves" who will emerge and not spare "the flock," and they will "draw away the disciples after them" (Acts 20:28-30). He warned the Ephesians about the possibility of Christians being "tossed to and fro by the waves and carried about by every wind of doctrine" (Ephesians 4:14).

Christians who live during the tribulation period must be discerning. The deceptive miracles of the false prophet will be enticing.

FREQUENTLY ASKED QUESTIONS

Will the false prophet be a Jew?

Some Bible expositors believe the false prophet will be a Jew because he is said to rise "out of the earth" (Revelation 13:11). Prophecy expert David Reagan comments, "Just as the sea is used symbolically in prophecy to refer to the Gentile nations, the land (or earth) is used to refer to Israel. This does not mean the false prophet will be an Orthodox Jew. It only means that he will be of Jewish heritage. Religiously, he will be an apostate Jew who will head up the One World Religion of the Antichrist."[25]

Other prophecy experts dispute the idea that the term "earth" indicates the false prophet's ethnic identity. The late John F. Walvoord, former president of Dallas Theological Seminary, explains it this way:

> While the first beast was a Gentile, since he came from the entire human race as symbolized by "the sea" (v. 1), the second beast was a creature of the earth. Some have taken this as a specific reference to the Promised Land and have argued that he was, therefore, a Jew. There is no support for this in the context, as the word for "earth" is the general word referring to the entire world. Actually, his nationality and geographic origin are not indicated.[26]

I think Walvoord is correct. However, there is room for debate among Christians on this issue. What we can all agree on is that the false prophet's primary purpose will be to exalt the antichrist.

Will the false prophet's Grade-B miracles
be impressive enough to deceive the entire world?

Yes. Allow me to call your attention to the words "performs great signs" in Revelation 13:13. The term *performs* is a present tense in the original Greek, indicating continuous action. The false prophet will engage in one Grade-B miracle after another. His supernatural feats will be ongoing. People will be impressed.

The biblical text describes these miracles as "great," which comes from the Greek word *megas*. This word is typically used of that which is great in the sense of outstanding, significant, important, or prominent. Even though they will be Grade-B miracles compared to God's Grade-A miracles, they will nevertheless be impressive. These miracles will be custom designed to deceive people (Revelation 13:14).

TODAY'S BIG IDEAS

- False prophets will proliferate during the end times, preparing the way for the ultimate false prophet, who will be the antichrist's right-hand man.

- The primary goal of the false prophet will be to move the world to worship the antichrist.

- Toward this end, the false prophet will perform many counterfeit signs and wonders. The amount of deception will be enormous.

TODAY'S TRANSFORMING TRUTHS

- Because Christians can be deceived (Ezekiel 34:1-7; Matthew 7:15-16; 24:4, 11; Acts 20:28-30; 2 Corinthians 11:2-3), it is imperative that we stockpile our minds with God's truth (2 Timothy 3:15-17). I recommend you follow a Bible reading plan. For example: Read John 1 on January 1; read John 2 on January 2; and so forth. *Make a plan and stick to it.*

- God calls every Christian to be "prepared to make a defense to anyone who asks" (1 Peter 3:15). We are to "destroy arguments and every lofty opinion raised against the knowledge of God" (2 Corinthians 10:5). We must "contend for the faith that was once for all delivered to the saints" (Jude 3). The apostle Paul set an example for us in "the defense and confirmation of the gospel" (Philippians 1:7). Don't be a secret-agent Christian. Ask God to embolden you to speak the truth.

Day 25

The Jewish Remnant
Flees Jerusalem

The abomination of desolation is portrayed in Jesus' Olivet Discourse as a huge warning sign that requires immediate action. Jesus urged:

> When you see the abomination of desolation spoken of by the prophet Daniel, standing in the holy place...then let those who are in Judea flee to the mountains. Let the one who is on the housetop not go down to take what is in his house, and let the one who is in the field not turn back to take his cloak. And alas for women who are pregnant and for those who are nursing infants in those days! Pray that your flight may not be in winter or on a Sabbath. For then there will be great tribulation, such as has not been from the beginning of the world until now, no, and never will be (Matthew 24:15-21).

When the antichrist desecrates the Jewish temple in Jerusalem, Jesus urges that the Jews living there should have no concern for their personal belongings. Their sole concern should be to get out of town with utmost speed. Time spent gathering belongings might mean the difference between life and death. Jesus warns that distress is about to escalate dramatically and rapidly.

The Jews who escape Jerusalem will flee to the deserts and mountains (Matthew 24:16), perhaps to Bozrah/Petra, about 80 miles south of Jerusalem. Others suggest Moab, Ammon, or Edom to the east. God promises to protect this remnant for the last three-and-a-half years of the tribulation period.

Revelation 12:13-17 provides the details:

> When the dragon saw that he had been thrown down to the earth, he pursued the woman who had given birth to the male child. But the woman was given the two wings of the great eagle so that she might fly from the serpent into the wilderness, to the place where she is to be nourished for a time, and times, and half a time. The serpent poured water like a river out of his mouth after the woman, to sweep her away with a flood. But the earth came to the help of the woman, and the earth opened its mouth and swallowed the river that the dragon had poured from his mouth. Then the dragon became furious with the woman and went off to make war on the rest of her offspring, on those who keep the commandments of God and hold to the testimony of Jesus.

➲ **The woman** in this passage represents Israel. The imagery is rooted in the Old Testament, where Israel is often viewed as the wife of God (Isaiah 54:5-6; Jeremiah 3:6-8; 31:32; Ezekiel 16:32; Hosea 2:16).

➲ **The male child** born of the woman (that is, *born of Israel*) is Jesus. (Jesus was of Jewish descent—Matthew 1:1; 2 Timothy 2:8; see also Romans 1:3; 9:4-5).

➲ **The dragon seeking to devour the child** likely alludes to the massacre of male children commanded by Herod (Revelation 12:4; Matthew 2:13-18; Luke 4:28-29). The devil was apparently behind these circumstances in his attempt to kill Jesus, and he was unsuccessful. Revelation 12:5 tells us that the "child" was ultimately "caught up to God"—that is, He ascended into heaven following His resurrection (Acts 1:9; 2:33; Hebrews 1:1-3; 12:2).

Satan—knowing he has very little time left (*just three-and-a-half years*)—seeks to persecute Israel (the Jews) with fury (Revelation 12:12-13). But God provides "two wings of the great eagle so that she might fly from the serpent into the wilderness" (Revelation 12:14). In the Bible, wings often represent protection and deliverance (Psalm 91:4; Isaiah 40:31). God once affirmed to the ancient Jews: "You yourselves have seen what I did to the Egyptians, and how I bore you on eagles' wings and brought you to myself" (Exodus 19:4). The "two wings" in Revelation 12:14 point to God's supernatural deliverance of a Jewish remnant.

God will preserve the Jews for "a time, times, and half a time." This refers to the last three-and-a-half years of the tribulation period (Daniel 7:25; 12:7). A *time* equals one year. *Times* equals two years. *Half a time* equals half a year.

Prophetic Scripture tells us that "the serpent poured water like a river out of his mouth after the woman, to sweep her away with a flood" (Revelation 12:15). Satan may cause a literal flood of water to dislodge and destroy the Jews. Or perhaps the flood is metaphorical, referring to a satanically driven army that will rapidly advance against the Jews. It could even refer to an outpouring of hatred—*anti-Semitism*.

Whatever the case, the earth, under God's providence, will come to the aid of the Jews (Revelation 12:16). If the flood is literal water, perhaps God will cause the ground to open up and swallow it. Likewise, if the flood is a rapidly advancing army, perhaps God will cause the ground to open up via a mighty earthquake to swallow up the attackers (Matthew 24:7; Revelation 6:12; 8:5; 11:13, 19; 16:18).

Never forget God's two promises to the Jews:

1. "No weapon that is fashioned against you shall succeed"—not even water, literal or metaphorical (Isaiah 54:17).
2. "He who keeps Israel will neither slumber nor sleep. The LORD is your keeper" (Psalm 121:4-5).

FAST FACTS ON SATAN'S ONGOING GOAL OF DESTROYING THE JEWS

Satan has persistently sought to destroy the Jews during both Old and New Testament times. Esau attempted to kill his brother Jacob, who would become the father of the 12 tribes of Israel. At the time Moses was born, the Egyptian pharaoh ordered the execution of all male Jewish babies born in Egypt. Israel would obviously not exist had Jacob or Moses not survived.

Haman plotted the extermination of the Jews. If it weren't for Esther's exposing of this hideous plot, the Jewish people might well have perished.

When Jesus was born, King Herod engaged in Jewish infanticide to attempt the murder of the babe Jesus. No wonder Jesus called Satan a "murderer from the beginning" (John 8:44). Satan was apparently behind all these murderous activities.

FREQUENTLY ASKED QUESTIONS

Is it possible that Satan's persecution and martyrdom of Jewish people during the tribulation period is engineered to prevent the second coming?

It is possible. Jesus will not return *until* the Jewish people are endangered at Armageddon, and *until* the Jewish leaders cry out for deliverance from the divine Messiah (Zechariah 12:10). In his perverted thinking, Satan may reason that if he can destroy the Jews, he can prevent their calling out to the divine Messiah and hence prevent the second coming of Christ, thus saving himself from defeat.

Is the antichrist's murderous attitude toward the Jews motivated by Satan?

I believe so. Second Thessalonians 2:9 tells us that the antichrist operates "by the activity of Satan." Revelation 13:2 tells us that Satan "gave his power" to the antichrist.

Just as Satan hates the Jews and wants to murder them, so the antichrist will hate the Jews and seek to murder them. Apparently Satan will persecute the Jews *through* the antichrist (Matthew 24:15-21).

Does the antichrist also target Christians during the tribulation period?

Most certainly! Revelation 13:7-10 tells us that the Satan-energized antichrist "was allowed to make war on the saints and to conquer them" (see also 2 Thessalonians 2:9). A parallel passage is Daniel 7:21, which reveals that the antichrist "made war with the saints and prevailed over them." Notice how these verses tell us that the antichrist will *conquer them* and *prevail over them*. Such language reveals there will be many martyrs among God's people during the tribulation period (Revelation 6:9-11).

TODAY'S BIG IDEAS

- The antichrist will desecrate the Jewish temple.
- This desecration will be a warning sign that catastrophic persecution against the Jews is imminent.
- Jesus therefore urges the Jews in Jerusalem to exit immediately and seek refuge in the wilderness, where God will providentially watch over the remnant.
- Large-scale persecution of Christians (the "saints") will also take place.

TODAY'S TRANSFORMING TRUTHS

- Though we are not yet in the tribulation period, Christians are nevertheless being targeted for persecution—even martyrdom—in some parts of the world. Even in countries with religious freedoms, Christians and Christian values are being ridiculed and ostracized. This is no time for Christians to succumb to the hideous disease known as *non-rocka-boatus*. We need bold Christians who avoid *contentiousness* but are well-equipped to *contend* for the faith (Jude 3). *Will you be one of these Christians?*
- God will providentially watch over the Jewish remnant during the second half of the tribulation period. By the word *providentially,* I am referring to "God's sovereignty with a purpose." You and I must learn to trust that God providentially watches over us as well (Psalm 23; Matthew 28:20; Hebrews 13:5). This is a great antidote for anxiety.

Day 26

The "Great Tribulation" Begins

The events of the second half of the tribulation period are so horrific that this period of time is appropriately labelled "the great tribulation." Before we address this, however, we must answer critics who claim we shouldn't divide the tribulation period into two parts.

The books of Daniel and Revelation provide good reasons for distinguishing the two halves of the tribulation period. Within the pivotal prophecy found in Daniel 9:27, we read of the antichrist: "He shall make a strong covenant with many for *one week*, and for *half of the week* he shall put an end to sacrifice and offering." The week refers to a week of years, or seven years. For half of that week—that is, for the last three-and-a-half years—the antichrist will put an end to animal sacrifices in the Jewish temple. The two halves of the tribulation period are clearly distinguished here.

God's two prophetic witnesses will minister on the earth for precisely 42 months (Revelation 11:2). They will prophesy for 1,260 days (verse 3). Both "42 months" and "1,260 days" refer precisely to three-and-a-half years. Their ministry will transpire during the first half of the tribulation period.

God will watch over the Jewish remnant in the wilderness for "a time, and times, and half a time" (Revelation 12:14). Recall, a *time* is a year; *times* refers to two years; and *half a time* refers to half a year. God will watch over the Jewish remnant for the last three-and-a-half years of the tribulation period—the *second half* of the tribulation.

Clearly, there are good scriptural reasons for distinguishing between the two halves of the tribulation period. There are also good reasons

supporting the idea that the second half of the tribulation will constitute the most horrific period of human suffering ever to hit planet Earth.

> So horrific is the second half of the tribulation period that it
> is labeled the **great tribulation** in Matthew 24:21-22.

Jesus, in His Olivet Discourse, speaks of the horror that begins at
the midpoint of the tribulation period: "Then there will be great tribulation, such as has not been from the beginning of the world until
now, no, and never will be. And if those days had not been cut short,
no human being would be saved. But for the sake of the elect those
days will be cut short" (Matthew 24:21-22; compare with Revelation
7:14). The prophet Daniel likewise speaks of the last half of the tribulation period, "There shall be a time of trouble, such as never has been
since there was a nation till that time" (Daniel 12:1).

Jeremiah 30:7 describes the severity of this time for Israel: "That day
is so great there is none like it; it is a time of distress for Jacob" (Jacob is
a metaphorical reference to Israel). The Amplified Bible translates the
verse, "That day is great, there is none like it; It is the time of Jacob's
[unequaled] trouble."

As for why the second half of the tribulation period is so "great,"
keep in mind all that happens during this second half:

- The Satan-inspired antichrist will persecute and martyr
  Jews with fury (Revelation 12:13, 17).

- The Satan-inspired antichrist will persecute and martyr
  Christians to such a degree that he will *conquer them* (Revelation 13:7-10) and *prevail over them* (Daniel 7:21).

- The bowl judgments will be unleashed—the most devast-
  ing of God's judgments (Revelation 16). These will involve
  horribly painful sores on human beings, bodies of water
  turning to blood, the death of all sea creatures, people
  being scorched by the sun, rivers drying up, total darkness

engulfing the land, a devastating earthquake, widespread destruction, and much more.

• Armageddon—a catastrophic war campaign—will be unleashed upon the world (Revelation 16:16). This will be an extended, escalating conflict, and the loss of life will be massive.

FAST FACTS ON GOD AS A PROTECTOR

Though the last three-and-a-half years of the tribulation period will be the great tribulation, God will protect the Jewish remnant in the wilderness during these years. Many verses in Scripture affirm God's role as the divine Protector: "You are a hiding place for me; you preserve me from trouble" (Psalm 32:7). "He will hide me in his shelter in the day of trouble; he will conceal me under the cover of his tent" (Psalm 27:5). "God is our refuge and strength, a very present help in trouble" (Psalm 46:1).

"Hide me from the secret plots of the wicked, from the throng of evildoers" (Psalm 64:2). "When you pass through the waters, I will be with you; and through the rivers, they shall not overwhelm you; when you walk through fire you shall not be burned, and the flame shall not consume you" (Isaiah 43:2).

Though the existential threat against the Jewish remnant will never be greater, God will providentially watch over and protect them. His plans for Israel will not be thwarted. God Himself proclaims, "I am God, and there is no other; I am God, and there is none like me, declaring the end from the beginning and from ancient times things not yet done, saying, My counsel shall stand, and I will accomplish all my purpose" (Isaiah 46:9-10).

FREQUENTLY ASKED QUESTIONS

How will the tribulation period be "shortened"?

Jesus affirmed about the great tribulation, "If those days had not been cut short, no human being would be saved. But for the sake of the elect those days will be cut short" (Matthew 24:21-22). Was Jesus saying He would make the great tribulation shorter than three-and-a-half years, or was He saying that three-and-a-half years is the shortened time?

To answer this question, we turn to the parallel verse in Mark 13:20: "If the Lord had not *cut short* the days, no human being would be saved. But for the sake of the elect, whom he chose, he *shortened* the days" (emphasis added). Greek scholars note that the two verbs in this verse—"cut short" and "shortened"—express action taken by God in the past. This means that God, in eternity past, sovereignly decreed a limitation on the length of the great tribulation.

What are God's sovereign decrees?

> **"The decrees** are God's eternal purpose. He does not make His plans or alter them as human history develops. He made them in eternity, and, because He is immutable, they remain unaltered (Ps. 33:11; James 1:17)."[27]

Jesus was thus teaching that God in eternity past decreed that the great tribulation would be shortened to precisely three-and-a-half years, and not a day more. God's prophetic plan involves a precise timetable.

How can a loving God allow the Jewish people to experience such a "great tribulation"?

God has a plan for national Israel. That plan includes allowing Israel to go through the great tribulation. During this period, God will purge Israel to motivate the nation to repent of its rejection of Jesus (Zechariah 13:8-9). At the very end of the tribulation period, a remnant of Jews will repent and turn to Jesus for salvation (Romans 9–11). Following the second coming, these redeemed Jews will be invited into Christ's millennial kingdom (Ezekiel 20:34-38). God will then fulfill all the promises He made to Israel. God will give Israel the land promised in the Abrahamic covenant (Genesis 12:1-3; 15:18-21; 17:21; 35:10-12). He will also fulfill the throne promise in the Davidic covenant, with Christ ruling on the throne of David throughout the millennial kingdom (2 Samuel 7:5-17).

I might summarize it this way: God loves His child Israel so much that He finds it necessary to punish this rebellious child so that the child will now behave properly. This behaving child will now be in a position to receive the magnificent blessings God has in store for her.

TODAY'S BIG IDEAS

- Prophetic Scripture distinguishes between the two halves of the tribulation period—especially in Daniel and Revelation.

- The last three-and-a-half years of the tribulation period are the "great tribulation." It will be a time of unrelenting travail.

- During this time, God will sovereignly protect the Jewish remnant hiding out in the wilderness.

- Mercifully, God has set a time limit on the great tribulation. It will last no longer than three-and-a-half years.

TODAY'S TRANSFORMING TRUTHS

- God sometimes has reasons for allowing His children to go through a "day of trouble." God allows us to experience trials because they are beneficial to us. First Peter 1:6-7 instructs us: "In this you rejoice, though now for a little while, if necessary, you have been grieved by various trials, so that the tested genuineness of your faith—more precious than gold that perishes though it is tested by fire—may be found to result in praise and glory and honor at the revelation of Jesus Christ." James 1:2-4 likewise tells us: "Count it all joy, my brothers, when you meet trials of various kinds, for you know that the testing of your faith produces steadfastness. And let steadfastness have its full effect, that you may be perfect and complete, lacking in nothing."

- When experiencing trials, let us remember that God can bring good out of evil: "We know that for those who love God all things work together for good, for those who are called according to his purpose" (Romans 8:28).

Day 27

The Mark of the Beast Is Enforced

At the midpoint of the tribulation period, the antichrist and the false prophet—a satanic, diabolical duo—will subjugate the entire world so that anyone who does not receive the mark of the beast will not be able to buy or sell. The false prophet will act on behalf of the antichrist and cause all, "both small and great, both rich and poor, both free and slave, to be marked on the right hand or the forehead, so that no one can buy or sell unless he has the mark, that is, the name of the beast or the number of its name" (Revelation 13:16-17). We are then told, "This calls for wisdom: let the one who has understanding calculate the number of the beast, for it is the number of a man, and his number is 666" (verse 18).

This means the false prophet will initiate a "squeeze play" by demanding that people worldwide receive the mark of the beast. He will effectively force people to make the following choice: *Either receive the mark and worship the antichrist or starve—with no ability to buy or sell.*

The antichrist's mark is a parody of God's sealing of the 144,000 witnesses of Revelation 7 and 14. Revelation 14:1 tells us that the 144,000 will have the names of the Lamb (Jesus) and the Father "written on their foreheads."

Receiving the mark of the beast constitutes an implicit approval of the antichrist as a leader and a tacit agreement with his purpose. No one will take this mark accidentally. One must volitionally choose to do so, with all the facts on the table. It will be a deliberate choice with eternal consequences. Those who choose to receive the mark will do so with the full knowledge of what they have done.

Human beings will somehow be branded, just as animals are today. The mark of the beast will indicate ownership and submission, religious commitment, and "religious orthodoxy" in submitting to the antichrist, who positions himself as God.

Notice how the domains of religion and economics become merged via the mark of the beast. One will depend on the other during the great tribulation. As David Jeremiah put it, "The mark will allow the antichrist's followers to buy and sell because it identifies them as religiously orthodox."[28] So, though receiving the mark is essentially a spiritual decision, it will have life-or-death economic consequences.

FAST FACTS ON "MARKS" DURING BIBLE TIMES

During Bible times, devotees of pagan religions received a tattoo as an emblem of ownership by a specific pagan deity. Slaves were branded by their masters, indicating ownership. Soldiers were branded by their military leaders, indicating allegiance to their commander.

The Greek word for "mark" (*charagma*) was also used to refer to the image of a Roman emperor on Roman coins. This image on the coins exalted the emperor.

In like manner, the beast's emblem will somehow be placed on people during the future great tribulation—just as marks were once placed on soldiers, slaves, and religious devotees. It will indicate allegiance and submission to the antichrist, as well as exalt the antichrist.

FREQUENTLY ASKED QUESTIONS

What is the significance of 666?

Revelation 13:18 tells us, "Let the one who has understanding calculate the number of the beast, for it is the number of a man, and his number is 666." Bible interpreters have struggled with the meaning of 666. A popular theory is that because the number seven is a number of perfection—and the number 777 is a number reflecting the perfect Trinity (Father, Son, and Holy Spirit)—perhaps 666 points to a being who aspires to perfect deity (like the Trinity), but never attains it. (The evil counterpart to the Trinity is the antichrist, the false prophet, and Satan.)

Others suggest that the number refers to a specific man—such as the Roman emperor Nero. When Nero's name is translated into the Hebrew language, the numerical value of its letters is 666.

All of this is highly speculative. Scripture does not clearly define what is meant by 666. Hence, interpreting this verse involves guesswork.

It is possible that we are not intended to know the meaning of 666 until the antichrist actually emerges on the world scene. The meaning of the number of his name may not be clear until he appears and fulfills the prophecy (see Revelation 13:18; 17:9; also see Daniel 9:22; 12:10).

How does modern technology relate to the mark of the beast?

The mark of the beast will involve a visible mark on the skin—perhaps a tattoo—that signifies allegiance to the antichrist. Revelation 13:16 explicitly states that the mark will be "on" the right hand or head.

Modern technology will enable the antichrist and false prophet to enforce the global economic system that is related to the mark of the beast. John F. Walvoord comments on how technology will make it possible for such economic control, based on whether people have received the mark: "There is no doubt that with today's technology, a world ruler, who is in total control, would have the ability to keep a continually updated census of all living persons and know day-by-day precisely which people had pledged their allegiance to him and received the mark and which had not."[29] Others have said it is highly likely that "chip implants, scan technology, and biometrics will be used as tools to enforce his policy that one cannot buy or sell without the mark."[30]

Does the mark of the beast hinge on a cashless world?

This is highly likely. And, significantly, certain aspects of our society have already gone cashless. Economists tell us that the amount of cash used today is less than half that used back in the 1970s. Why so? Because more and more people are using cashless options—credit cards, debit cards, Apple Pay, Android Pay, and others.

Presently, more than 70 percent of all consumer payments are done electronically. Economists say cash could soon become obsolete. Bills and coins will be relegated to the history books. Retail establishments may soon begin charging surcharges every time a customer tries to use cash in their establishments.

A cashless system—perhaps involving an international cryptocurrency—would make it very easy for the antichrist to control who can buy and sell during the tribulation period. With today's strong trend toward a cashless world, the stage is being set for the mark of the beast.

Does receiving the mark of the beast carry eternal consequences?

Yes. Receiving the mark of the beast—in conjunction with worshiping the beast—is an unpardonable sin. Revelation 14:9-10 affirms: "If anyone worships the beast and its image and receives a mark on his forehead or on his hand, he also will drink the wine of God's wrath, poured full strength into the cup of his anger, and he will be tormented with fire and sulfur in the presence of the holy angels and in the presence of the Lamb."

Such words are sobering. Anyone who expresses loyalty to the antichrist and his cause will suffer the wrath of our holy and just God. How awful it will be for these people to experience the full force of God's divine anger and unmitigated vengeance (see Psalm 75:8; Isaiah 51:17; Jeremiah 25:15-16)! By contrast, those who have believed in the Lord Jesus Christ, and who have refused the mark of the beast, will come to life and reign with Christ for 1,000 years (Revelation 20:4).

TODAY'S BIG IDEAS

- The false prophet will force the mark of the beast on people worldwide during the second half of the tribulation period.

- The mark will indicate submission and commitment to the antichrist.

- No one will be able to buy or sell without the mark. It will be a "passport to commerce."

- Those who receive the mark, and worship the beast, are destined for God's wrath.

TODAY'S TRANSFORMING TRUTHS

- Jesus urged, "Do not lay up for yourselves treasures on earth, where moth and rust destroy and where thieves break in and steal, but lay up for yourselves treasures in heaven, where neither moth nor rust destroys and where thieves do not break in and steal. For where your treasure is, there your heart will be also" (Matthew 6:19-21; see also John 6:27). We must never compromise a relationship with God for the sake of material concerns. Heavenly treasures ought to take priority, even if it means going hungry, or going through a degree of temporal suffering.

- Unlike those during the tribulation period who will receive the mark of the beast, you and I have the mark of the Holy Spirit—that is, the "seal" of the Holy Spirit (Ephesians 1:13; 4:30). A *seal* indicates possession and security. God "possesses" believers as His children and He will see them securely into heaven. *Praise the Lord!*

The Seven Bowl Judgments Are Unleashed

Scripture reveals there will be "seven angels with seven plagues, which are the last, for with them the wrath of God is finished" (Revelation 15:1). Just as God uses angels in the unleashing of the seal and trumpet judgments, so angels will be used in the unleashing of the bowl judgments. These angels do God's bidding (see Psalm 103:20).

> The **bowl judgments** will be the worst—*and the last*—judgments that fall upon the world during the tribulation period.

The bowl judgments are similar in some ways to the plagues God inflicted upon the Egyptians at the hands of Moses. Just as God severely judged the ancient Egyptians, so God will now severely judge the God-rejecting inhabitants of the earth.

As the *last* judgments, they are the worst of all, and are unleashed toward the end of the seven-year tribulation period. They unfold rapidly, with each new judgment worse than the former. These bowl judgments can be viewed as an escalating crescendo of horrors.

The seven golden bowls are said to be full of the wrath of God. Such wrath is appropriate for a God-rejecting and unrepentant world (Revelation 15:7). Woe unto any human beings who live on the earth at this time.

Here's how it all begins: A loud voice—probably that of God Himself—will proclaim, "Go and pour out on the earth the seven bowls" (Revelation 16:1). The first four bowl judgments target individuals on the earth and lead to increasing misery. The last three judgments are more international and lead to the war campaign of Armageddon.

FAST FACTS ON THE SEVEN BOWL JUDGMENTS

The first angel will pour out his bowl (Revelation 16:2). The result is that painful sores will come upon people loyal to the antichrist. The Greek word for "sores" carries the idea of skin ulcers on the surface of the body. Some Bible expositors suggest this could come about as a result of radiation poisoning from nuclear weapons that might be detonated. (Revelation 8:7 tells us that "a third of the earth was burned up, and a third of the trees were burned up, and all green grass was burned up.") However, God can also easily inflict painful sores directly, as He did during Old Testament times.

The second angel will pour out his bowl (Revelation 16:3). The sea will become like blood, leading to the total death and extinction of sea creatures. In contrast to the second trumpet judgment, where the waters turn into blood and one-third of the sea creatures die (Revelation 8:8-9), the present judgment causes *virtually all* life in the sea to be destroyed. This brings to mind God's judgment against the Egyptians when the Nile was turned into blood (Exodus 7:17-21).

The third angel will pour out his bowl (Revelation 16:4). The rivers and springs of water will become blood, just like the sea. This is particularly devastating because there will now be no remaining freshwater sources. When God turned the Nile into blood, the people "could not drink the water of the Nile" (Exodus 7:24; Psalm 78:44). People can live for a time without food, but they can't live long without water.

The fourth angel will pour out his bowl upon the sun (Revelation 16:8). The intensity of the sun's heat will be significantly increased so that it scorches those who dwell on the earth (compare with Isaiah 24:6; 42:25; Malachi 4:1). It is possible that with all the other judgments that have affected the environment during the tribulation period, the ozone layer may become so depleted and thin that the sun's rays become much more intense. The combination of a scorching-hot sun and no fresh water to drink will lead to immense misery. People will curse the name of God and refuse to repent (Revelation 16:9). Just as Pharaoh's heart hardened as judgments fell against Egypt (Exodus 7:13-14, 22; 8:15, 19, 32; 9:7, 34-35; 13:15), so the people of the tribulation will harden their hearts against God (Psalm 95:8; Ephesians 4:18).

The fifth angel will pour out his bowl on the throne of the beast (Revelation 16:10). God here judges the dominion of the antichrist, and all who follow him. The antichrist's kingdom will be "plunged into darkness." People will gnaw their tongues, curse God, and refuse repentance (verses 10-11). These people will choose to continue their loyalty to the antichrist instead of turning to the one true God of heaven who can bring relief. Their minds will continue to be blinded by the power of Satan (2 Corinthians 4:4).

The sixth angel will pour out his bowl on the great river Euphrates (Revelation 16:12). This river is strategic. It is the primary water boundary between the Holy Land and the rest of Asia to the east. Asian kings and their armies will be aided on their march toward Armageddon by the supernatural drying up of the river. These Asian kings will probably think their suffering is due to the God of Israel. They may think that attacking the Jews will constitute an attack against God Himself. Revelation 16:13 reveals that demons will summon kings from all over the earth to participate in Armageddon (Revelation 16:14).

In the chronology of Revelation, the seventh bowl judgment in Revelation 16:17-21 follows the second coming of Christ. We see this by comparing Revelation 16 to other prophetic verses. For this reason, I will hold off addressing the seventh bowl judgment until I first address the second coming. (Everything will make better sense this way.) Here, I will simply note that the seventh bowl judgment will bring an end to God's judgments during the tribulation period.

FREQUENTLY ASKED QUESTIONS

What is Armageddon?

Armageddon is a catastrophic war campaign that occurs at the end of the tribulation period (Daniel 11:40-45; Joel 3:9-17; Zechariah 14:1-3; Revelation 16:14-16).

> **Armageddon** literally means "Mount of Megiddo" and refers to a location about 60 miles north of Jerusalem. This was the location of Barak's battle with the Canaanites (Judges 4) and Gideon's battle with the Midianites (Judges 7). This will be the site for the final horrific battles of humankind just before the second coming of Jesus Christ (Revelation 16:16).

Napoleon is reported to have once said that this site is perhaps the most significant battlefield he had ever seen. Of course, the battles Napoleon fought will dim in comparison to Armageddon. So horrible will Armageddon be that no one would survive if it were not for Christ coming again (Matthew 24:22). Jesus prophesied about Armageddon and mentioned that birds would have a feast on the battlefield: "Wherever the corpse is, there the vultures will gather" (Matthew 24:28; Luke 17:37). The scene will be gruesome.

How can people's minds become so twisted that they refuse to turn from sin so that things will get better for them?

A primary factor is that human beings are fallen in sin. They have a bent toward evil. Every aspect of their being—including their minds—is fallen in sin (see Genesis 6:5; Jeremiah 17:9; Romans 7:18).

To use an analogy, buggy software can cause a computer to crash. Likewise, buggy thinking—sinful thoughts in the mind—can cause human beings to "crash" in the sense that they make wrong choices.

This reminds me of Psalms 1 and 2. Psalm 1:2 tells us that the blessed person is one who perpetually meditates on God's law. This is in contrast to the ungodly "imaginings" of unbelievers: "Why do...the people imagine a vain thing?" (Psalm 2:1 KJV). The words *meditate* and *imagine* are translations of the same Hebrew word. While believers meditate on God and His Word, unbelievers meditate on sinful things—including reasons to refuse repentance in the face of God's judgments (Revelation 16:9, 11). Their imaginings truly are vain!

TODAY'S BIG IDEAS

- The first bowl judgment will result in harmful sores coming upon people loyal to the antichrist.
- The second bowl judgment will result in the sea becoming like blood, leading to the total death and extinction of sea creatures.
- The third bowl judgment will result in the rivers and springs of water becoming blood, just like the sea. There will be no remaining freshwater sources.
- The fourth bowl judgment will result in the sun's heat intensifying so that the people of the earth are scorched.
- The fifth bowl judgment will be against the antichrist's throne and will result in his kingdom being plunged into darkness.
- The sixth bowl judgment will result in the Euphrates River drying up, enabling easy passage for the armies of the East en route to their participation in Armageddon.
- The seventh bowl judgment—which follows the second coming—will result in the completion of God's wrath being poured out upon the world.
- Despite the horror of these woes from God's hand, people's hearts will continue to harden.

TODAY'S TRANSFORMING TRUTHS

- This is a great time to express thanks to God for delivering the church from the wrath to come (1 Thessalonians 1:10; 5:9; Revelation 3:10). This deliverance will come at the rapture, which precedes the tribulation period.
- The hearts of sinners during the tribulation period will grow harder and harder against God. Let us beware of the scriptural teaching that even Christians can develop hard or calloused hearts (Psalm 95:8; Hebrews 3:8, 15). The formula for avoiding a hard heart is simple: *Trust God and obey Him* (Hebrews 4).

Day 29

Armageddon Begins: Commercial New Babylon Is Destroyed

A major shift will take place at the midpoint of the tribulation period. The antichrist will destroy religious New Babylon. He will execute God's two prophetic witnesses. He will claim to be God and enthrone himself in the Jewish temple. Both Jews and Christians will be targeted for intense persecution and martyrdom throughout the second half of the tribulation. Meanwhile, the antichrist will wield control of the world economy via the mark of the beast. This will continue right up till the end of the tribulation.

We've already witnessed a steady escalation of human suffering throughout the tribulation period. First are the seal judgments, involving bloodshed, famine, death, economic upheaval, a great earthquake, and cosmic disturbances (Revelation 6). Then come the trumpet judgments, involving hail and fire mixed with blood, the sea turning to blood, water turning bitter, further cosmic disturbances, affliction by demonic scorpions, and the death of a third of humankind (Revelation 8:6–9:21). Then come the bowl judgments, involving painful sores on human beings, more bodies of water turning to blood, the death of all sea creatures, people being scorched by the sun, total darkness engulfing the land, a devastating earthquake, and much more (Revelation 16).

Worse comes to worst, however, when already-traumatized human beings find themselves amid a catastrophic war campaign called Armageddon (Daniel 11:40-45; Joel 3:9-17; Zechariah 14:1-3; Revelation 16:14-16). This will take place at the very end of the tribulation period. Millions of people will perish in the worst escalation of conflict ever to hit earth.

Given all that occurs at Armageddon, it would be wrong to refer to it as the "battle" of Armageddon, as if it were a single event. Armageddon will involve an extended, escalating conflict. And it will be catastrophic.

Armageddon will begin with the allied armies of the antichrist gathering for the ultimate destruction of the Jews (Revelation 16:12-16). Demonic spirits will go "abroad to the kings of the whole world, to assemble them for battle on the great day of God the Almighty."

At the initial phase of Armageddon, commercial New Babylon will be destroyed by attackers.

> **New Babylon** will be a worldwide economic center during the second half of the tribulation period. Its influence will be universal. It will have an octopus-like reach around the world. Because of the commercial success of this city, merchants around the world will become wealthy. Anti-God materialism will run rampant.

Because of God's wrath, Babylon will become "an utter desolation; everyone who passes by Babylon shall be appalled, and hiss because of all her wounds" (Jeremiah 50:13). "How Babylon has become a horror among the nations! I set a snare for you and you were taken, O Babylon, and you did not know it; you were found and caught, because you opposed the LORD. The LORD has opened his armory and brought out the weapons of his wrath" (verses 23-25).

Isaiah 13:19 informs us that Babylon's destruction "will be like Sodom and Gomorrah when God overthrew them." Jeremiah 50:40 likewise says of Babylon's destruction: "As when God overthrew Sodom and Gomorrah and their neighboring cities, declares the LORD, so no man shall dwell there, and no son of man shall sojourn in her."

The book of Revelation is graphic in its description of New Babylon's destruction:

> A mighty angel took up a stone like a great millstone and threw it into the sea, saying, "So will Babylon the great city be thrown down with violence, and will be found no more;

and the sound of harpists and musicians, of flute players and trumpeters, will be heard in you no more, and a craftsman of any craft will be found in you no more, and the sound of the mill will be heard in you no more, and the light of a lamp will shine in you no more, and the voice of bridegroom and bride will be heard in you no more, for your merchants were the great ones of the earth, and all nations were deceived by your sorcery. And in her was found the blood of prophets and of saints, and of all who have been slain on earth" (Revelation 18:21-24).

FAST FACTS ON DOUBLE-JUDGMENT

Speaking of God's judgment of New Babylon, a voice from heaven affirms, "Her sins are heaped high as heaven, and God has remembered her iniquities. Pay her back as she herself has paid back others, and repay her double for her deeds" (Revelation 18:5-6).

Here we find an echo of the *lex talionis*, the law of retaliation. As Matthew 7:2 says: "For with the judgment you pronounce you will be judged, and with the measure you use it will be measured to you." Galatians 6:7 assures us, "Whatever one sows, that will he also reap." In Babylon's case, the city will receive a double dose of *lex talionis*. To pay back double was a common judicial requirement in Old Testament law:

> If the stolen beast is found alive in his possession, whether it is an ox or a donkey or a sheep, he shall pay double (Exodus 22:4).

> If a man gives to his neighbor money or goods to keep safe, and it is stolen from the man's house, then, if the thief is found, he shall pay double (Exodus 22:7).

> For every breach of trust, whether it is for an ox, for a donkey, for a sheep, for a cloak, or for any kind of lost thing, of which one says, "This is it," the case of both parties shall

come before God. The one whom God condemns shall pay double to his neighbor (Exodus 22:9).

Speak tenderly to Jerusalem, and cry to her that her warfare is ended, that her iniquity is pardoned, that she has received from the LORD's hand double for all her sins (Isaiah 40:2).

I will doubly repay their iniquity and their sin, because they have polluted my land with the carcasses of their detestable idols, and have filled my inheritance with their abominations (Jeremiah 16:18).

Bring upon them the day of disaster; destroy them with double destruction! (Jeremiah 17:18).

In keeping with God's longstanding policy, Babylon's judgment will be thorough—that is, *double*! New Babylon will not survive this judgment.

FREQUENTLY ASKED QUESTIONS

Who will the attackers of New Babylon be?

The attack will come from a military coalition in the north. Jeremiah 50 instructs us: "For behold, I am stirring up and bringing against Babylon a gathering of great nations, from the north country. And they shall array themselves against her...Behold, a people comes from the north; a mighty nation and many kings are stirring from the farthest parts of the earth...They are cruel and have no mercy. The sound of them is like the roaring of the sea" (verses 9, 41-42). We are not informed of the specific identities of the northern invaders.

Just as the Babylonians were used during Old Testament times as God's rod of judgment against Israel, He will use a northern coalition as His whipping rod against Babylon. Just as Babylon showed no mercy in its oppression of Israel, so God will now show no mercy to Babylon.

Scripture reveals that when New Babylon is destroyed during the end of the tribulation period, the antichrist will not be present in the city. He will be told of its destruction by messengers (Jeremiah 50:43; 51:31-32).

How will the world respond upon witnessing the destruction of New Babylon?

The rulers of the world will grieve. They will lament when they witness the collapse of the economic system that enabled them to live so luxuriously (Revelation 18:9-20). The collapse of New Babylon means the luxurious empire of the antichrist is doomed forever.

Can you clarify the chronology of religious New Babylon's fall versus commercial New Babylon's fall?

The antichrist and his forces will destroy the false religion associated with New Babylon at the midpoint of the tribulation period (Revelation 17). The destruction of commercial New Babylon will take place at the end of the seven-year tribulation period at the hands of a northern coalition (Revelation 18).

TODAY'S BIG IDEAS

- The campaign of Armageddon—an extended time of severe conflict—will erupt at the end of the tribulation period. Millions of people will perish in the worst escalation of conflict ever to hit earth.

- The allied armies of the antichrist will gather for the ultimate destruction of the Jews.

- Before the attack against the Jews, New Babylon will be destroyed and will become desolate. The entire world will grieve at the sight of New Babylon's annihilation.

TODAY'S TRANSFORMING TRUTHS

- Prior to New Babylon's destruction, God instructs believers, "Come out of her, my people, lest you take part in her sins, lest you share in her plagues" (Revelation 18:4). This reminds me of 2 Corinthians 6:17: "Therefore go out from their midst, and be separate from them, says the Lord." God calls His people to separate from evil. Ask the Lord to reveal to you any areas in your life where there may yet be compromise in regard to evil.

- It is wise to live by the principle that God blesses the humble but brings down the prideful (Philippians 2:3; Colossians 3:12; James 4:6). How hard the prideful fall. New Babylon is a graphic example.

- While God said He would not forget New Babylon's sins (Revelation 18:5), He also said He purposefully forgets the sins of His children: "I will forgive their iniquity, and I will remember their sin no more" (Jeremiah 31:34; see also Hebrews 8:12). Rejoice and be glad in this!

Day 30

Armageddon Continues: The Jews Are Targeted for Destruction

Armageddon begins with the allied armies of the antichrist gathering for the ultimate destruction of the Jews (Revelation 16:12-16). Soon after this gathering, New Babylon—the commercial headquarters of the antichrist during the second half of the tribulation period—will be destroyed by a northern coalition.

Even the destruction of the antichrist's capital will not be enough to distract him away from his primary goal of destroying the Jewish people. Hence, instead of launching a counterattack against the northern military coalition that wiped out Babylon, the antichrist and his forces will move south to attack Jerusalem.

Two pivotal passages on the antichrist's attack against Jerusalem—Zechariah 12:1-3 and 14:1-2—reveal that *all the nations of the world* will gather against Jerusalem. Because "all the nations" will be gathered, the United States must be among that group. It seems likely that following the rapture of the church, the United States will become an ally of the antichrist. Jerusalem will fall and be ravaged in the face of this overwhelming onslaught.

Of course, not all the Jews will be in Jerusalem when the antichrist and his forces attack. We recall that at the midpoint of the tribulation period, the antichrist will break his covenant with Israel and exalt himself as deity, even putting an image of himself within the Jewish temple. In Jesus' Olivet Discourse, He warned of how quickly the Jews must flee for their lives out of Jerusalem when those things occur (Matthew 24:16-31). Many Jews will escape to the deserts and mountains (Matthew 24:16), perhaps to Bozrah/Petra, about 80 miles south of Jerusalem.

This escape from Jerusalem is described in Revelation 12:6: "The woman [a metaphor referring to Israel] fled into the wilderness, where she has a place prepared by God, in which she is to be nourished for 1,260 days" (insert added for clarity). Indeed, "the woman was given the two wings of the great eagle so that she might fly from the serpent into the wilderness, to the place where she is to be nourished for a time, and times, and half a time" (verse 14). This verse means that God will enable the Jews to escape quickly, and He will take care of them for three-and-a-half years—a *time* (year), *times* (two years), and *half a time* (half a year).

It is this remnant of Jews in the wilderness that the antichrist now targets near the end of the seven-year tribulation. These Jews sense impending doom as the antichrist's forces gather in the rugged wilderness, poised to attack to eradicate them. They are helpless, and—from an earthly perspective—utterly defenseless. At this strategic juncture, God will remove the spiritual blindness of the remnant. The Jews will trust in Jesus for salvation, and then call out to their new Messiah for deliverance from the antichrist's forces.

FAST FACTS ON THE REMNANT'S CONVERSION TO CHRIST

The Jewish leaders will call for the Jews to repent. Their collective repentance will take two days: "Come, let us return to the LORD; for he has torn us, that he may heal us; he has struck us down, and he will bind us up. After two days he will revive us; on the third day he will raise us up, that we may live before him" (Hosea 6:1-2).

The Jewish leaders of the first century AD led the Jewish people to reject Jesus as their Messiah. Now, however, the Jewish leaders will urge repentance and instruct all to turn to Jesus as their Messiah. This, the remnant will do, and they will be saved. This fulfills the prophecy of Joel 2:28-29 that there will be a spiritual awakening of the Jewish remnant.

The restoration of Israel will include the confession of Israel's national sin (Leviticus 26:40-42; Jeremiah 3:11-18; Hosea 5:15), after which the remnant will become saved. This fulfills the apostle Paul's prophecy of Israel's redemption in Romans 11:25-27.

Now, in dire threat at Armageddon, the Jews will plead for their newly found Messiah to return and deliver them (Zechariah 12:10; Matthew 23:37-39), at which point their deliverance will come (Romans 10:13-14). The divine Messiah promptly returns at the second coming to rescue the Jewish remnant from danger. (Chapter 31 will provide full details on the second coming.)

FREQUENTLY ASKED QUESTIONS

Will many Jews lose their lives during the tribulation period?

Sadly, yes. Zechariah 13:7-9 informs us that two-thirds of the Jewish people will lose their lives during the tribulation period. However, one-third—the remnant—will survive and turn to the Lord and be saved (see Isaiah 64:1-12). This represents a severe purging of unbelieving Israel and prepares the way for the remnant to finally turn to the Lord for salvation.

Later, in the millennial kingdom, Israel (the Jewish remnant) will experience full possession of the promised land (Genesis 12:1-3; 15:18-21; 17:21; 35:10-12) and the reestablishment of the Davidic throne (2 Samuel 7:5-17). It will be a time of physical and spiritual blessing, the basis of which is the new covenant (Jeremiah 31:31-34).

Why did God inflict a judgment of judicial blindness upon Israel in the first place?

The apostle Paul informs us, "I do not want you to be unaware of this mystery, brothers: a partial hardening has come upon Israel, until the fullness of the Gentiles has come in" (Romans 11:25)—that is, until the full number of Gentiles who will be saved have, in fact, become saved.

The backdrop is that Israel had sought a relationship with God via a righteousness earned by keeping the law. Instead of seeking a faith-relationship with God, through Christ, they instead sought to do everything that the law prescribed so they could earn a relationship with God in that way (see Galatians 2:16; 3:2, 5, 10).

Failure was unavoidable, for no human being can attain righteousness by observing the law (James 2:10). To make matters worse, they rejected Jesus as the Messiah-Savior, refusing to turn to Him in faith because He did not fit their preconceived ideas about the Messiah (Matthew 12:14, 24).

God thus inflicted partial judicial blindness or hardness of heart upon Israel in judgment. Israel thus lost her favored position before God, and the gospel was then preached to the Gentiles, with a view to causing the Jews to become jealous and then become saved (Romans 11:11). Israel's hardening and casting off was always intended to be a temporary measure that would lead to Israel's salvation.

Fast-forward to the campaign of Armageddon. The armies of the antichrist are now gathered in the desert wilderness, poised to attack the Jewish remnant. Things appear to be desperate.

Something extraordinary will then happen. In His grace and mercy, God will remove the judicial spiritual blindness that He inflicted upon the Jews following their rejection of Jesus as the promised Messiah (Romans 9–11). Once their blindness has been removed, the Jews in the wilderness will promptly repent of their rejection of Jesus and believe in Him as their divine Messiah. They will call to their new Lord for rescue from the antichrist, and the second coming of Christ will promptly take place.

Does this mean the second coming of Christ is a "rescue mission"?

Yes, it is. Prophecy scholar Thomas Ice explains it this way: "Many Christians are surprised to learn that the second coming is a rescue event. Jesus will return to planet earth in order to rescue the believing Jewish remnant that is on the verge of being destroyed during the Campaign of Armageddon. I think this is what Paul speaks of in Romans 10 when he tells us, 'Whoever will call upon the name of the Lord will be saved'...the Jewish people are going to have to be Believers in Jesus as their Messiah in order to be rescued by Him at the second advent. This is exactly what will happen."[31]

TODAY'S BIG IDEAS

- In the campaign of Armageddon, Jerusalem will fall and be ravaged by the antichrist's forces.

- The antichrist and his forces will then move south to attack the Jewish remnant in the wilderness.

- The Jewish remnant will be endangered, being hopelessly outnumbered by the vast forces of the antichrist.

- In his perfect sovereign timing, God will remove the judicial blindness from the Jewish remnant.

- The remnant will then experience national regeneration and call out to their Messiah for deliverance from the antichrist's forces.

- Jesus Christ will return in glory and rescue the Jewish remnant.

TODAY'S TRANSFORMING TRUTHS

- Just as the antichrist will target the Jews, so Satan—who is much more powerful—now targets Christians. Just as the Jews will find deliverance by calling upon Jesus Christ, so you and I can find deliverance by calling upon Jesus Christ. It is good to remember that the sheep who are the safest from the wolf are those who stay nearest the Shepherd (Psalm 23; John 10:1-18).

- The Jewish remnant under siege will feel helpless in the face of the overwhelming forces of the antichrist. Have you ever felt helpless in the face of overwhelming circumstances? Never forget that God is "a stronghold to the needy in his distress" (Isaiah 25:4). "The LORD is near to the brokenhearted and saves the crushed in spirit" (Psalm 34:18). "God is our refuge and strength, a very present help in trouble" (Psalm 46:1).

Day 31

The Glorious Appearing
of Jesus Christ

The Jews, having become believers in the Lord Jesus, will cry out to Him for deliverance from the approaching forces of the antichrist (Zechariah 12:10; Matthew 23:37-39; Romans 11:25-27). Jesus will promptly answer their prayers and return to rescue the remnant. Every eye will see Him (Revelation 1:7). Christ will come as the King of kings and Lord of lords. No one will be able to withstand Him (Revelation 19:11-16). The antichrist's forces will be as nothing in the face of His Eternal Royal Majesty.

The second coming is described in glorious terms in Revelation 19:11-16:

> I saw heaven opened, and behold, a white horse! The one sitting on it is called Faithful and True, and in righteousness he judges and makes war. His eyes are like a flame of fire, and on his head are many diadems, and he has a name written that no one knows but himself. He is clothed in a robe dipped in blood, and the name by which he is called is The Word of God. And the armies of heaven, arrayed in fine linen, white and pure, were following him on white horses. From his mouth comes a sharp sword with which to strike down the nations, and he will rule them with a rod of iron. He will tread the winepress of the fury of the wrath of God the Almighty. On his robe and on his thigh he has a name written, King of kings and Lord of lords.

Christ riding the white horse will be the glorious Commander-in-Chief of heaven's armies. It signifies His coming in triumph over the forces of wickedness in the world. This contrasts with the lowly colt Jesus rode during His first coming (see Zechariah 9:9; Mark 11:1-11).

> Jesus is called **Faithful and True** in this context because He is returning to earth in glory *just as He promised* He would (Matthew 24:27-31). He said He'd come, and now He is here!

Christ's eyes are like a flame of fire. This points not only to His absolute holiness but to His penetrating scrutiny in seeing all things as they truly are (Revelation 1:14). At the second coming, no one will escape His omniscient gaze.

On Jesus' head "are many diadems" (Revelation 19:12). These crowns represent total sovereignty and royal kingship. No one will challenge Christ's kingly authority. The "armies of heaven"—both angelic and previously raptured Christians—will accompany Christ back to earth.

> Jesus is called **King of kings and Lord of lords** (Revelation 19:16). This title means that Jesus is supreme and sovereign over all earthly rulers and angelic powers (1 Timothy 6:15; see also Deuteronomy 10:17; Psalm 136:3). No one can challenge His rule.

In His Olivet Discourse, Jesus spoke about how people in the world will be woefully unprepared for His second coming. It will be much like the days of Noah, with people partying it up, unconcerned about spiritual matters (Matthew 24:37-40). Jesus then stressed the need for watchfulness and readiness among His people: You must be ready, "for the Son of Man is coming at an hour you do not expect" (Matthew 24:42-44).

FAST FACTS ON JESUS' KINGSHIP

Genesis 49:10 prophesied that the Messiah would come from the tribe of Judah and reign as a king. In Psalm 2:6, God the Father announces the installation of God the Son as King in Jerusalem. Psalm 110 affirms that the Messiah will subjugate His enemies and rule over them. Daniel 7:13-14 tells us that the Messiah-King will have an everlasting dominion. Revelation 19:16 speaks of Jesus as the "King of kings and Lord of lords." The Davidic covenant in 2 Samuel 7:16 promises a Messiah who would have a dynasty, a people over whom He would rule, and an eternal throne (see also Luke 1:32-33). Jesus will reign on the throne of David during the millennial kingdom.

FREQUENTLY ASKED QUESTIONS

Why does it sometimes seem as if the second coming is being delayed?

Second Peter 3:9 instructs us: "The Lord is not slow to fulfill his promise as some count slowness, but is patient toward you, not wishing that any should perish, but that all should reach repentance." God is patiently waiting for people to repent. Of course, time is running out. Once Jesus comes, there is no further opportunity to repent and turn to Him.

This is in keeping with God's long track record of immense patience before bringing people to judgment (see Joel 2:13; Luke 15:20; Romans 9:22). We should not be surprised that He continues this patience in the present age.

What is the sign of the Son of Man?

In His Olivet Discourse, Jesus said, "Then will appear in heaven the sign of the Son of Man, and then all the tribes of the earth will mourn, and they will see the Son of Man coming on the clouds of heaven with power and great glory" (Matthew 24:30).

Bible expositors disagree over what might be meant by "the sign of the Son of Man." Some suggest the sign of the cross will appear in the sky for all to see. Others suggest it refers to the lightning that "flashes in the east and shines to the west" (Matthew 24:27 NLT). Others suggest that perhaps it is the glory of Christ that will be powerfully manifest at the second coming. Still others choose not to define the sign, affirming that the main thing is that Christ Himself will return visibly. Maybe the Son of Man *Himself* is the sign (see Daniel 7:13; Acts 1:11; Revelation 19:11-21).

Why will "all the tribes of the earth" mourn when Christ comes in glory (Matthew 24:30)?

There may be several aspects of this mourning. On the one hand, just before the second coming, the Jewish remnant—now living in the wilderness—will finally come to see that Jesus is indeed the divine Messiah, and these Jews will finally trust in Christ for salvation. They will mourn over their previous foolish rejection of the Messiah (see Zechariah 12:10-12). On the other hand, people worldwide who have been living in open defiance and rebellion against God throughout the tribulation period will mourn because they recognize that the divine Judge is now here, and it's time to face the consequences of their rebellion.

Was Jesus wrong when He said in the first century AD, "Behold, I am coming soon" (Revelation 22:7)?

Bible expositors explain Jesus' assertion in different ways. Some suggest that from a human perspective, Jesus' return may not have come soon, but from a divine perspective, it will. We have been in the last days since the incarnation of Christ (Hebrews 1:2; James 5:3). James 5:9 affirms that "the Judge is standing at the door." Romans 13:12 exhorts us that "the night is far gone; the day is at hand." First Peter 4:7 warns, "The end of all things is at hand." Given such verses, Christ is coming "soon" from the divine perspective.

Other scholars suggest that perhaps Jesus meant He was coming soon from the perspective of the events described in the book of Revelation. From the vantage point of those living during the tribulation period itself, Christ is coming soon.

Still others say that the main idea in these words is that the coming of Christ is imminent. This being the case, we must all be ready, for we do not know precisely when He will return.

Is it possible Christ might be ashamed of me at the second coming?

Jesus gave a sobering warning to His followers in Luke 9:26: "Whoever is ashamed of me and of my words, of him will the Son of Man be ashamed when he comes in his glory and the glory of the Father and of the holy angels" (compare with 1 John 2:28). A Christian who, in some fashion, acts ashamed of Jesus will not lose his or her salvation, but may be met with shame at the second coming. This goes hand in hand with the reality that Christians who do not live fully committed lives may suffer the loss of some rewards at the judgment seat of Christ (1 Corinthians 3:10-15; 2 Corinthians 5:10).

TODAY'S BIG IDEAS

- Christ will physically and visibly come again.
- Christ will come again as the King of kings and Lord of lords.
- Christ will rescue the Jewish remnant from the forces of the antichrist. (I will provide further details on this in the next chapter.)
- Many people living during the tribulation period will be unprepared for the second coming.

TODAY'S TRANSFORMING TRUTHS

- Jesus is the sovereign "King of kings and Lord of lords" (Revelation 19:16). Given this truth, it is good to engage in periodic self-examination (2 Corinthians 13:5). Ask yourself: Is Christ presently enthroned upon my heart? Is there anything I am holding back from my King and Lord? *The place of blessing in the Christian life is the place of complete surrender and submission.*
- Jesus is called "Faithful and True" (Revelation 19:11). Because He is faithful and true, *we can trust everything He has said in Scripture.* Because He is faithful and true, *we can trust Him with all the circumstances of our lives.*

Day 32

The Final Battle
of Armageddon Erupts

At His second coming, Christ will confront the antichrist and his formidable forces, and slay them with the word of His mouth. The enemies of Christ will suffer instant defeat when they face Christ, the omnipotent King of kings and the Lord of Lords:

> The armies of heaven, arrayed in fine linen, white and pure, were following him on white horses. From his mouth comes a sharp sword with which to strike down the nations, and he will rule them with a rod of iron. He will tread the winepress of the fury of the wrath of God the Almighty. On his robe and on his thigh he has a name written, King of kings and Lord of lords (Revelation 19:14-16).

The contextual backdrop is that the antichrist and his forces will be poised to launch an attack against the Jewish remnant in the wilderness. The remnant will have no chance of survival. God—according to His perfect timing—will remove the spiritual blindness of the Jewish people. The Jewish leaders will urge them to repent and believe in Jesus the Messiah. Upon believing in Him, they will call out to Him for deliverance from the forces of the antichrist. Then the second coming of Christ will promptly occur.

Armies (plural) will accompany Christ from heaven to earth (Revelation 19:14):

⮑ **One army will be angelic.** Jesus Himself tells us, "The Son of Man is going to come with his angels in the glory of his Father" (Matthew 16:27). "When the Son of Man comes in his glory, and all the angels with him, then he will sit on his glorious throne" (25:31).

⮑ **The other army will comprise redeemed human beings.** They are "arrayed in fine linen, white and pure" (Revelation 19:14). This is the image used to describe the wedding gown of the bride of Christ, which is the church (Revelation 19:8).

How glorious it will be! Christ will lead both holy angels and redeemed humans in a massive entourage to earth.

Upon Christ's arrival to earth, judgment will fall on His enemies. From Christ's mouth "comes a sharp sword with which to strike down the nations" (Revelation 19:15). The sharp sword symbolizes Christ's omnipotent power to execute His enemies (see Isaiah 11:4). Since the sword is portrayed as coming out of His mouth, Christ likely accomplishes His victory over His enemies by His spoken word. Just as Christ created the universe by speaking (Psalm 33:6; Colossians 1:16; John 1:3), so the enemies of God will meet their end by the power of Christ's spoken word.

What this means, in popular vernacular, is that Jesus will essentially say, "Drop dead," and the forces of the antichrist will experience instant death. Their attack against His chosen people will yield a complete forfeiture of their lives.

Try to picture this in your mind. As the formidable forces of the antichrist advance on the relatively small Jewish remnant, the Jews will plead for their newly found Messiah to return and deliver them (Zechariah 12:10). Christ will respond by immediately leaving heaven with His entourage of two armies. When the antichrist surmises that

Christ is coming, he will prepare for battle: "The beast and the kings of the earth with their armies gathered to make war against him who was sitting on the horse and against his army" (Revelation 19:19). The forces of the antichrist are enormous, from all over the earth, and they are hopeful that their collective strength will be enough to overcome Christ. When Christ arrives to earth, however, He merely speaks the word and they all drop dead.

Second Thessalonians 2:8 speaks of the antichrist, "whom the Lord Jesus will kill with the breath of his mouth and bring to nothing by the appearance of his coming." The Jewish Messiah will obliterate all opposition. The antichrist's forces will be destroyed from Bozrah all the way back to Jerusalem (Joel 3:12-13; Zechariah 14:12-15; Revelation 14:19-20).

Jesus will then victoriously descend to the Mount of Olives. We read about this in Zechariah 14:3-4:

> On that day his feet shall stand on the Mount of Olives that lies before Jerusalem on the east, and the Mount of Olives shall be split in two from east to west by a very wide valley, so that one half of the Mount shall move northward, and the other half southward.

At this juncture, right at the end of the tribulation period, we finally witness the unleashing of the seventh bowl judgment:

> The seventh angel poured out his bowl into the air, and a loud voice came out of the temple, from the throne, saying, "It is done!" And there were flashes of lightning, rumblings, peals of thunder, and a great earthquake such as there had never been since man was on the earth, so great was that earthquake. The great city was split into three parts, and the cities of the nations fell, and God remembered Babylon the great, to make her drain the cup of the wine of the fury of his wrath. And every island fled away, and no mountains were to be found. And great hailstones, about one hundred pounds each, fell from heaven on people; and they cursed God for the plague of the hail, because the plague was so severe (Revelation 16:17-21).

Cataclysmic events will bring an end to the tribulation period. However, judgments of human beings still remain on the horizon—the judgment of the Gentile nations (Matthew 25) and the judgment of the Jews (Ezekiel 20). Both judgments will precede Christ's millennial kingdom. Those found to be believers among the Gentiles and Jews will enter Christ's kingdom. Those found to be unbelievers will be cast into judgment.

FAST FACTS ON THE END OF THE TIMES OF THE GENTILES

The term "**times of the Gentiles**" refers to an extended time of Gentile domination over Jerusalem (Luke 21:24).

This extended period began with the Babylonian captivity of the Jewish people that started in 605 BC. Throughout biblical history, Babylon, the Medo-Persian Empire, Greece, and Rome were the dominant powers over Jerusalem. All of this constitutes the "times of the Gentiles."

Daniel 2:44 prophesies the end of Gentile dominion over Jerusalem: "The God of heaven will set up a kingdom that will never be destroyed or conquered. It will crush all these kingdoms into nothingness, and it will stand forever" (NLT). This means Christ will overthrow all earthly kingdoms and, following the second coming, will set up His own millennial kingdom that will last 1,000 years on earth (Revelation 20:4). Once the millennial kingdom ends, Christ will continue His reign forever in the eternal state.

The times of the Gentiles will thus not cease until the end of the great tribulation, when Christ comes again. The antichrist and his global empire that has run roughshod over Jerusalem will be divinely terminated (Daniel 2:35, 45; Revelation 19:20; 20:10). This will finally and definitively put an end to the times of the Gentiles (Luke 21:24, 27).

FREQUENTLY ASKED QUESTIONS

Do "armies" accompany Christ because He needs them to defeat the antichrist?

By no means. It is Christ alone—as omnipotent God, the King of kings and Lord of lords, the eternal Potentate—who will engage in battle against the enemies of God. These armies accompany Christ to participate in the events that follow the second coming, including the establishment of Christ's millennial kingdom (Revelation 20:4; 1 Corinthians 6:2; 2 Timothy 2:12).

What does Scripture mean when it says Christ "will tread the winepress of the fury of the wrath of God the Almighty" (Revelation 19:15)?

During biblical days, grapes were squeezed to get the grape juice out, which was then used to produce wine. This "squeezing" took place by putting the grapes into small vats with special floors angled toward container jars. Hired workers would tread upon the grapes with their bare feet, causing the juice to flow into the jars. This treading upon grapes became a common metaphor for judgment during Bible times. However, instead of grape juice flowing, the blood of unbelievers will flow when Christ slays them.

TODAY'S BIG IDEAS

- Jesus Christ will return in glory and rescue the Jewish remnant.

- The final battle will erupt—but the battle ends up not being a battle at all. Christ will instantly destroy all the antichrist's forces.

- Christ will victoriously descend to the Mount of Olives.

- With the cataclysmic seventh bowl judgment, the tribulation period will end.

TODAY'S TRANSFORMING TRUTHS

- From the perspective of the relatively small Jewish remnant, the problem they face is insurmountable. The international forces of the antichrist all but guarantee their demise. Let's learn a lesson: *God is always bigger than our problems, regardless of how immense those problems may appear.* God can come through for us against all odds.

- During the tribulation period, some believers may be mind-boggled to witness the unleashing of the escalating judgments of God. You may be mind-boggled by some of your own circumstances. Here is what has helped me in the past: When bad things occur around me that I don't understand, that is the most important time to anchor myself on the things *I do* understand. And what *I do* understand is that while I may be ignorant of the ultimate outcome of my circumstances, I do know the One who is in control of my circumstances—and He is my anchor!

Day 33

The 75-Day Interim Between the Tribulation and the Millennium

There will be a 75-day interim between the end of the tribulation period and the beginning of the millennial kingdom. We infer this interim based on the following biblical facts:

- Daniel 12:12 states, "Blessed is he who waits and arrives at the 1,335 days."
- The second half of the tribulation period is three-and-a-half years, which is 1,260 days.
- This means Daniel's 1,335 days extend 75 days beyond the end of the tribulation period.
- The math is simple: 1,335 minus 1,260 equals 75.

Since the millennial kingdom has not yet begun, we conclude there is a 75-day interim between the end of the tribulation period and the beginning of the millennial kingdom. Several prophetic events occur during this interim, including the judgment of the nations, the judgment of the Jews, a marriage feast for the divine Groom (Jesus) and His bride (the church), and preparations for the beginning of the millennial kingdom. Let's briefly consider each of these.

The Judgment of the Nations. Believers and unbelievers from among the Gentile nations are pictured as sheep and goats (Matthew 25:31-46). They are intermingled and require separation by a special judgment. The sheep (believers) will enter Christ's 1,000-year millennial kingdom. The goats (unbelievers) will depart into eternal punishment.

The judgment of the nations will determine which individual Gentiles are believers. They will be permitted entrance into Christ's millennial kingdom.

Christ will judge the Gentiles based on how they treated His "brothers" during the tribulation period. In Christ's reckoning, treating His brothers kindly is the same as treating Him kindly. Treating His brothers with contempt is the same as treating Him with contempt.

Comparing this passage with the details of the tribulation period suggests that the "brothers" are the 144,000 Jewish evangelists mentioned in Revelation 7 and 14. These are Christ's Jewish brothers who faithfully bear witness of Him during the tribulation.

Even though the antichrist and the false prophet will wield economic control over the world during this period (Revelation 13), God will still be at work. God's redeemed (the sheep) will come to the aid of Christ's Jewish brethren with food and water (and meet other needs) as these Jews bear witness to Christ all around the globe.

The saved Gentiles (the sheep) will enter the millennial kingdom in their mortal bodies and continue to get married and have children throughout the millennium. They will not yet receive glorified/resurrected bodies. Although longevity will characterize the millennial kingdom, mortal Gentiles will continue to age and die (Isaiah 65:20). They will be resurrected following the millennial kingdom (Revelation 20:4-5).

The Judgment of the Jews. Christ will also judge the Jews during the 75-day interim (Ezekiel 20:34-38). The Lord will gather the Jews from all around the earth to Israel and then purge all the rebels—those who refused to turn to Him for salvation. Believers among the gathered Jews will be invited to enter Christ's millennial kingdom. They will enjoy the blessings of the new covenant, the Davidic covenant, and the Abrahamic covenant (Jeremiah 31:31; Ezekiel 20:37).

Like their Gentile counterparts, these saved Jews will not yet receive glorified/resurrected bodies. They will enter the kingdom in their mortal bodies and continue to get married and have children through-out the millennium (Matthew 25:46). Because longevity will charac-terize the millennial kingdom, they will mature to a nice old age, but they will eventually die (Isaiah 65:20). They will be resurrected follow-ing the millennium (Revelation 20:4-5).

The Marriage Feast of the Lamb. Scripture often speaks of the relation-ship between Christ and the church using a marriage motif, with Christ being the divine Bridegroom and the church being the bride (Matthew 9:15; 25:1-13; Mark 2:19-20; Luke 5:34-35; John 3:29).

> **Traditional Hebrew weddings** conclude with a marriage feast. Jesus and the church will have a marriage ceremony in heaven (Revelation 19:7-16). Following the second coming, the marriage feast will then be celebrated during the 75-day interim (verse 9). It will be an incredible spectacle.

Final Preparations for the Millennial Kingdom. Final preparations for the millennial kingdom will also be made during the 75-day interim. Scripture reveals four specific preparations:

1. The antichrist and the false prophet will no longer be permitted to attack God's people. They will be cast alive into the lake of fire (Revelation 19:20).

2. Satan will be bound in the bottomless pit for 1,000 years (Revelation 20:2).

3. Christ will set up the governmental structure of the millennial kingdom (2 Timothy 2:12; Revelation 20:4-6). Faithful Christians will reign with Christ, and He will undoubtedly hand out governmental assignments.

4. Tribulation saints martyred by the antichrist will be resurrected from the dead. They, too, will participate in reigning with Christ for a thousand years (Revelation 20:4).

FAST FACTS ON METAPHORS FOR THE CHURCH

A variety of metaphors are used in the New Testament to describe the church. The church is the bride of Christ (Revelation 21:2), a "new man" (Ephesians 2:15), the body of Christ (Colossians 1:18), the temple of the Holy Spirit (1 Corinthians 3:16), and God's household (Ephesians 2:19-20; 1 Timothy 3:14-15).

FAST FACTS ON REIGNING WITH CHRIST

- Believers are a kingdom of priests and will reign with Christ—Revelation 5:10; 20:6.
- If we endure, we will reign with Christ—2 Timothy 2:12.
- Christ's martyrs will reign with Him—Revelation 20:4.
- Overcoming Christians will sit on the throne with Christ—Revelation 3:21. (Elsewhere in Scripture, we see that "conquering" and "overcoming" are essentially synonyms for faithfulness and obedience [Revelation 2:11, 17, 26; 3:5, 12].)
- Christ's servants will reign forever—Revelation 22:5.

FREQUENTLY ASKED QUESTIONS

What does Scripture say about the close connection between Jesus Christ and His followers?

Matthew 25:31-46 reveals that treating Christ's brothers kindly is the same as treating Him kindly. Treating His brothers with contempt is the same as treating Him with contempt. Other verses point to this same close connection between Christ and His followers. Recall that Saul was a persecutor of Christ's followers. When Jesus appeared to him on the road to Damascus, He asked him: "Saul, Saul, why are you persecuting me?" (Acts 9:4). Jesus likewise told His followers, "Whoever receives you receives me, and whoever receives me receives him who sent me" (Matthew 10:40). He also said, "The one who hears you hears me, and the one who rejects you rejects me, and the one who rejects me rejects him who sent me" (Luke 10:16). The apostle Paul instructed the Corinthian Christians, "Sinning against your brothers and wounding their conscience when it is weak, you sin against Christ" (1 Corinthians 8:12). Christ thus viewed His followers as being intimately connected with Him.

Is the judgment of the nations the same as the great white throne judgment?

Scripture portrays these as two different judgments:

Different Time: The judgment of the nations occurs at the second coming of Christ (Matthew 25:31); the great white throne judgment occurs following the millennial kingdom (Revelation 20:11-12).

Different Scene: The judgment of the nations occurs on earth (Matthew 25:31); the great white throne judgment occurs, of course, at the great white throne (Revelation 20:11).

Different Subjects: The judgment of the nations involves three groups of people: the sheep, the goats, and the brothers (Matthew 25:32, 40). The great white throne judgment involves only the unsaved dead from all of time (Revelation 20:12).

Different Bodies: No resurrection occurs in connection with the judgment of the nations. However, a resurrection occurs before the great white throne judgment (Revelation 20:13).

Different Basis: The basis of judgment at the judgment of the nations is how Christ's "brothers" are treated (Matthew 25:40). The basis of judgment at the great white throne judgment is works throughout earthly life (Revelation 20:12).

Different Result: The result of the judgment of the nations is twofold: the righteous enter into Christ's millennial kingdom and the unrighteous are cast into the lake of fire. The great white throne judgment results in the wicked dead being cast into the lake of fire. The righteous are not mentioned because they are not there.

We conclude that these are two different judgments.

TODAY'S BIG IDEAS

During a 75-day interim between the end of the tribulation period and the beginning of the millennial kingdom, Jesus will:

- Judge the Gentile nations, after which Gentile believers will be invited into the millennial kingdom;
- judge the Jews, after which Jewish believers will be invited into the millennial kingdom;
- celebrate a marriage feast with His "bride" (the previously raptured church); and
- make governmental assignments among His followers for the smooth operation of the millennial kingdom.
- Also during this time, the antichrist and the false prophet will be captured and cast into the lake of fire, permanently ending their harassment of God's people;
- a mighty angel will incarcerate Satan in the bottomless pit, where he will remain quarantined for 1,000 years.

TODAY'S TRANSFORMING TRUTHS

- As members of the church (the bride of Christ), we presently await the coming of the Groom (Christ) to take us to the place He has prepared for us in the Father's house. While we wait, we are called to live in fidelity to our Groom (Matthew 25:23; Luke 16:10; 1 Corinthians 16:13; Philippians 1:27; 2 Timothy 3:14; Revelation 2:10).
- In view of what you have learned about the close connection between Christ and His followers (Matthew 10:40; 25:31-46; Luke 10:16; Acts 9:4), does that change the way you want to treat your brothers and sisters in Christ? Are there any relationships in need of restoration?

Day 34

The Millennial Kingdom Begins

Following the second coming of Christ and the 75-day interim, Jesus will set up His kingdom on earth. This is known in theological circles as "the millennial kingdom" (Revelation 20:2-7).

> **Millennium** comes from two Latin words—*mille*, which means "thousand," and *annum*, which means "year." The millennial kingdom will last 1,000 years.

I noted in the previous chapter that the Gentiles will face Christ at the judgment of the nations (Matthew 25:31-46), while the Jews will face Christ at a separate judgment (Ezekiel 20:34-38). These occur during the 75-day interim. Only those found to be believers in both groups will be invited into the millennial kingdom in their mortal bodies (Matthew 25:34, 46).

Married couples among both groups will continue to have children throughout the millennium. And while people will live much longer during the millennium than they do today, mortal Jews and Gentiles will continue to age and die (Isaiah 65:20). They will be resurrected at the end of the millennium (Revelation 20:4).

The good news for the Jews is that after thousands of years, God's covenant promises to Israel will finally be fulfilled in the millennial kingdom. The land promises in the Abrahamic covenant will be fulfilled (Genesis 15:18-21; 26:3-4; 28:13-14). The throne promises in the Davidic covenant will be fulfilled, with Christ reigning upon the throne of David (2 Samuel 7:12-16). The promise of Israel's regeneration and spiritual empowerment in the new covenant will also be fulfilled (Jeremiah 31:31-34).

A unique feature of the millennial kingdom is that a new temple will be built (Ezekiel 40–48). The millennial temple will be the final temple for Israel. The dimensions provided for this temple make it significantly larger than any other temple in Israel's history.

This large temple will represent God's presence among His people during the millennium (Ezekiel 37:26-27). It will be a worship center of Jesus Christ during that time. Even redeemed Gentiles will worship within it (Isaiah 60:6; Zephaniah 3:10; Zechariah 2:11).

FAST FACTS ON CHRIST'S MILLENNIAL RULE

Some have wrongly concluded that Christ's future rule in the millennial kingdom is addressed *only* in the Davidic covenant (2 Samuel 7:12-13). In truth, His rule is confirmed in many passages apart from the covenant:

- "May he have dominion from sea to sea, and from the River to the ends of the earth!" (Psalm 72:8).

- "To us a child is born, to us a son is given; and the government shall be upon his shoulder, and his name shall be called Wonderful Counselor, Mighty God, Everlasting Father, Prince of Peace. Of the increase of his government and of peace there will be no end, on the throne of David and over his kingdom, to establish it and to uphold it with justice and with righteousness from this time forth and forevermore. The zeal of the LORD of hosts will do this" (Isaiah 9:6-7).

- "I saw in the night visions, and behold, with the clouds of heaven there came one like a son of man, and he came to the Ancient of Days and was presented before him. And to him was given dominion and glory and a kingdom, that all peoples, nations, and languages should serve him; his dominion is an everlasting dominion, which shall not pass away, and his kingdom one that shall not be destroyed" (Daniel 7:13-14).

- "He shall speak peace to the nations; his rule shall be from sea to sea, and from the River to the ends of the earth" (Zechariah 9:10).

FAST FACTS ON THREE PROPHETIC COVENANTS

I addressed the biblical covenants at the beginning of the book. It is appropriate that we briefly revisit them here because these covenants *are the very foundation of the millennial kingdom.* If not for these pivotal covenants, the millennial kingdom would make little sense!

1. *The Abrahamic Covenant.* God long ago made land promises to Abraham involving specific boundaries (Genesis 15:18-21). The land promises were then passed down through Isaac's line (Genesis 26:3-4) and Jacob's line (Genesis 28:13-14). Psalm 105:8-11 affirms that this covenant is "an everlasting covenant." The land will finally be given to Israel at the outset of the millennial kingdom.

2. *The Davidic Covenant.* God made a covenant with David in which He promised that one of his descendants would rule forever on the throne of David (2 Samuel 7:12-13; 22:51). This covenant will find its fulfillment in Jesus Christ, born from the line of David (Matthew 1:1), who will rule during the millennial kingdom (Ezekiel 36:1-12; Micah 4:1-5; Zephaniah 3:14-20; Zechariah 14:1-21).

3. *The New Covenant.* This covenant promises the internal power for the Jews to obey God's commands. It promises a complete national regeneration of Israel, and every Jew in the millennial kingdom—bar none—will know the Lord (Isaiah 44:1-5; Jeremiah 24:7; Ezekiel 11:19-20; 36:25-27; Joel 2:28-32; Romans 11:25-27). Gentile believers also share in the spiritual benefits of the new covenant.

FREQUENTLY ASKED QUESTIONS

How do we know only believers enter the millennial kingdom?

Daniel informs us that only the saints enter the kingdom: "The saints of the Most High shall receive the kingdom and possess the kingdom...The time came when the saints possessed the kingdom" (Daniel 7:18, 22).

> The word "**saint**" in Daniel is from an Aramaic word derived from a Hebrew root, *Oilp*. This word has the connotation of a divine claim and ownership of the person. It connotes that which is distinct from the common or profane. So, only those who are God's people—those "owned" by God—enter into the kingdom.

It is inconceivable that the wicked and the saints could together inherit a kingdom universally characterized by righteousness (Isaiah 61:11), peace (Isaiah 2:4), holiness (Isaiah 4:3-4), and justice (Isaiah 9:7). The parable of the wheat and weeds (Matthew 13:30), as well as the parable of the good and bad fish (Matthew 13:49-50), confirm that only the saved go into the kingdom.

Will the children of all the believers who enter the millennial kingdom also become believers?

No. While only saints enter the kingdom, some of their children, grandchildren, and great-grandchildren (and the like) *will not* become believers. Some will grow to adulthood rejecting the Savior-King in their hearts, even though they render outward obedience in the kingdom. Some of these people will eventually participate in the final revolt against God at the end of the millennium. Satan will be released from the abyss and lead a host of rebellious humans in this final revolt against God (Revelation 20:7-8).

Why will there be animal sacrifices in the millennial kingdom?

Some Bible expositors have surmised that the millennial sacrifices will be a Jewish memorial of the awful price Christ—the Lamb of God—had to pay for the salvation of people. The temple system will thus allegedly function much like the Lord's Supper does today, as a memorial ritual (1 Corinthians 11:25-26; see also Isaiah 56:7; 66:20-23; Jeremiah 33:17-18; Ezekiel 43:18-27; 45:13-25; 46:24; Malachi 3:3-4).

The problem with this viewpoint is that Ezekiel says the sacrifices are "to make atonement" (Ezekiel 45:15, 17, 20). Hence, the "memorial" viewpoint seems to fall short of explaining these sacrifices.

The solution may be that the purpose of the sacrifices in the millennial temple is to remove ceremonial uncleanness and prevent defilement from polluting the purity of the temple environment. According to this view, such ceremonial cleansing of the temple will be necessary because Yahweh will again dwell on the earth amid sinful (and therefore unclean) mortal people. (Remember, these people survive the tribulation period and enter the millennial kingdom in their mortal bodies—still retaining their sinful natures, even though redeemed by Christ as believers.) The sacrifices will thus remove any ceremonial uncleanness in the temple.

> The **sacrifices in the millennial temple** cannot and should not be seen as a return to the Mosaic law. The law has forever been done away with through Jesus Christ (Romans 6:14-15; 7:1-6; 1 Corinthians 9:20-21; 2 Corinthians 3:7-11; Galatians 4:1-7; 5:18; Hebrews 8:13; 10:1-14). The sacrifices relate only to removing ritual impurities in the temple, as fallen-though-redeemed human beings remain on earth.

TODAY'S BIG IDEAS

- Following the second coming of Christ and the 75-day interim, Jesus will set up His millennial kingdom on earth. It will last 1,000 years.

- All who became believers during the tribulation period will enter the millennial kingdom—both Jew and Gentile.

- God's covenant promises to Israel will finally be fulfilled in the millennial kingdom. This includes the land promises in the Abrahamic covenant, the throne promises in the Davidic covenant, and the promises of Israel's regeneration and spiritual empowerment in the new covenant.

- A unique feature of the millennial kingdom will be the presence of a temple.

TODAY'S TRANSFORMING TRUTHS

- Have you ever thought about how important it is that God is a promise keeper (Numbers 23:19; Joshua 21:45; 1 Kings 8:56)? The fulfillment of the biblical covenants is just one illustration of God as a promise keeper. God will also honor all the countless scriptural promises relating to our wondrous salvation in Christ. *Give thanks to the Lord!*

- Christ's millennial rule is *yet future*. But Christ's heart-rule over our lives is *present tense*. It's a reality now. Let's double up on our efforts to be fully submissive to King Jesus (John 8:31; 14:23-24; 15:10-15). Hold nothing back!

Day 35

Physical and Spiritual Blessings During the Millennium

The redeemed who enter Christ's millennial kingdom will enjoy both physical and spiritual blessings. People will live in a blessed and enhanced environment. Even the desert will blossom richly with vegetation, and the terrain will be unimaginably beautiful (Isaiah 35:1-2). There will be plenty of rain for the ground and food for animals roaming the countryside (Isaiah 30:23-24; 35:7). *Everything will be perfect.*

Animals will live in harmony with each other and with human beings. Their predatory and carnivorous natures will be removed (Isaiah 11:6-7).

People will live much longer than they presently do: "No more shall there be in it an infant who lives but a few days, or an old man who does not fill out his days, for the young man shall die a hundred years old" (Isaiah 65:20).

Say goodbye to the healthcare industry because there will be no further need for it. Physical infirmities and illnesses will be removed: "In that day the deaf shall hear the words of a book, and out of their gloom and darkness the eyes of the blind shall see" (Isaiah 29:18). "And no inhabitant will say, 'I am sick'" (Isaiah 33:24).

Prosperity will prevail all over the world, resulting in great joy and gladness:

> They shall be radiant over the goodness of the LORD, over the grain, the wine, and the oil, and over the young of the flock and the herd; their life shall be like a watered garden, and they shall languish no more. Then shall the young women rejoice in the dance, and the young men and the old shall be merry. I will turn their mourning into joy; I will comfort them, and give them gladness for sorrow...My

people shall be satisfied with my goodness, declares the LORD (Jeremiah 31:12-14).

These and many other physical blessings will be abundantly present during the future millennial kingdom. *How awesome it will be!*

Christ will also bring great spiritual blessings to those who live in the millennial kingdom. All these spiritual blessings relate to the wonderful reality that Christ Himself will be present with His people on earth.

The prophet Isaiah proclaims that "the earth shall be full of the knowledge of the LORD as the waters cover the sea" (Isaiah 11:9). When one combines this with the reality that Satan will be bound during the millennial kingdom (Revelation 20:1-3), we can scarcely imagine the depth of spiritual blessings that will prevail on earth during this time.

The spiritual blessings people will enjoy are based on the new covenant (Jeremiah 31:31-34). As an outworking of this wondrous covenant, abundant spiritual blessings will shower the earth. For example, the Holy Spirit will be present and will indwell all believers (Ezekiel 36:27; 37:14). Righteousness will prevail worldwide (Isaiah 46:13; 51:5; 60:21), as will obedience to the Lord (Psalm 22:27; Jeremiah 31:33), holiness (Isaiah 35:8-10; Joel 3:17), faithfulness (Psalm 85:10-11; Zechariah 8:3), and unified worship of the Messiah (Zephaniah 3:9; Zechariah 8:23; Malachi 1:11). God's presence will be made manifest throughout the earth (Ezekiel 37:27-28; Zechariah 2:10-13).

FAST FACTS ON DIFFERENT VIEWS OF THE MILLENNIUM

There are three views of the millennium:

➲ **Amillennialism** takes a metaphorical approach. It says there will be no literal millennial kingdom. Prophetic verses related to the reign of Christ metaphorically refer to Christ's present spiritual rule from heaven during the church age.

⊃ **Postmillennialism** also takes a metaphorical approach. It holds that through the church's progressive influence, the world will become "Christianized" before Christ returns. The kingdom of God is allegedly now being extended in the world through the preaching of the gospel.

⊃ **Premillennialism** teaches that following the second coming, Christ will institute a kingdom of perfect peace and righteousness that will last for 1,000 years.

I believe premillennialism is the correct view for the following reasons:

1. Premillennialism naturally emerges from a literal approach to prophecy.

2. This view best explains the unconditional land promises made to Abraham and his descendants, which are yet to be fulfilled (Genesis 13:14-18; Deuteronomy 30).

3. This view makes the best sense of the unconditional Davidic covenant in regard to the throne promise (2 Samuel 7:12-16).

4. This view is consistent with the Old Testament ending with a firm expectation of the messianic kingdom (for example, Isaiah 9:6; 16:5; Malachi 3:1).

5. This view best explains the scriptural teaching that Jesus and the apostles would reign on thrones in Jerusalem (Matthew 19:28; 25:31-34).

6. This view is most consistent with the apostle Paul's promise that Israel will one day be restored (Romans 9:3-4; 11:1).

FREQUENTLY ASKED QUESTIONS

If Satan is locked up during the millennial kingdom, what about demons?

In Revelation 20:1-3, the apostle John specifies that Satan will be imprisoned in the abyss during the millennial kingdom so he cannot "deceive the nations any longer." Even though this prophetic text mentions only Satan, it is likely that demons will also be incarcerated during this time. Several scriptural facts support this view.

We know that the fallen angels are subject to Satan, and they serve his ends. Revelation 12:7 thus refers to "the dragon and his angels" (see also Matthew 12:41). The "messenger of Satan" who afflicted Paul is an example of a demon doing Satan's bidding (2 Corinthians 12:7). Here's why this is significant: If Satan were locked up during the millennium—but the demons were still free—they could *do his bidding on the earth*. I don't think God would allow that.

We also know that Satan is not a "Lone Ranger" when it comes to deception. Fallen angels deceive too. We read about "teachings of demons" in 1 Timothy 4:1. This points to the need to "test the spirits" (1 John 4:1). Such verses indicate that people on earth are deceived not just by Satan but also by fallen angels who do Satan's bidding.

The purpose of Satan's incarceration during the millennial kingdom is so that he might not "deceive the nations any longer" (Revelation 20:3). If Satan's angels (demons) were still on the loose, the nations would surely still be subject to deception. One might therefore infer that Satan's fallen angels will also be locked up to prevent such deception.

We also know that the millennial kingdom will be characterized by great spiritual blessing—worldwide righteousness, obedience to the Lord, holiness, faithfulness, and unified worship. It is hard to see how all this could be a reality on earth with fallen angels still on the loose.

What are the implications of Satan and demons no longer being around during the millennial kingdom?

Satan will no longer accuse believers' consciences regarding their failures (Revelation 12:10). He will no longer take adversarial positions against them (1 Peter 5:8), and no longer spread deception as the father of lies (John 8:44).

Satan will no longer influence the world as the "god of this age" (2 Corinthians 4:4 NIV) or as "the prince of this world" (John 12:31 NIV). He will no longer function as a "roaring lion" who seeks to devour believers (1 Peter 5:8-9), and he will no longer tempt them into evil (Matthew 4:3; Acts 5:3; 1 Corinthians 7:5; Ephesians 2:1-3; 1 Thessalonians 3:5).

Satan will no longer hinder the work of believers (1 Thessalonians 2:18), wage war against them (Ephesians 6:11-12), sow weeds among them (Matthew 13:38-39), incite persecution against them (Revelation 2:10), and plant doubt in their minds (Genesis 3:1-5). He will no longer foster spiritual pride in the hearts of believers (1 Timothy 3:6) and will no longer lead them away from "the simplicity and purity of devotion to Christ" (2 Corinthians 11:3 NASB1995). Demons will no longer hinder answers to the prayers of believers (Daniel 10:12-20) and will no longer instigate jealousy and faction among them (James 3:13-16).

TODAY'S BIG IDEAS

- During the millennial kingdom, people will live in a blessed and enhanced environment.
- Animals will live in harmony with each other and human beings.
- People will live much longer than they presently do. Physical infirmities and illnesses will be removed.
- Prosperity will prevail worldwide, resulting in great joy and gladness.
- Christ will bring great spiritual blessing to His millennial kingdom—primarily rooted in the fact that Jesus will be present with His people. The Holy Spirit's presence will be pervasive.
- Righteousness, obedience to the Lord, holiness, faithfulness, and unified worship of the Messiah will prevail.

TODAY'S TRANSFORMING TRUTHS

- The Holy Spirit will pour out great spiritual blessing on the inhabitants of the millennial kingdom (Ezekiel 36:27; 37:14). But we need not wait until the millennial kingdom to be blessed by the Holy Spirit. Even now, we can walk in dependence on the Holy Spirit and obtain victory over sin (Galatians 5:16-21). We can enjoy and manifest the fruit of the Holy Spirit (Galatians 5:22-25) and minister to others through the spiritual gift(s) the Holy Spirit gives us (Romans 12:6-8; 1 Corinthians 12:7-10, 28-30).
- Obedience to God will prevail during the millennial kingdom (Psalm 22:27; Jeremiah 31:33). But we need not wait until the millennial kingdom to enjoy the benefits of obedience to God, which brings long life (1 Kings 3:14; John 8:51), happiness (Psalm 112:1; 119:56), peace (Proverbs 1:33), and a state of well-being (Jeremiah 7:23). *I want those blessings, don't you?*

Day 36

Satan's Final Revolt
After the Millennium

The devil—and likely the fallen angels who do his bidding—will be bound in the bottomless pit for 1,000 years during Christ's millennial kingdom (Revelation 20:1-3). This quarantine will effectively remove a powerfully destructive and deceptive force in all areas of human life and thought during Christ's millennial kingdom.

> The **bottomless pit**, also known as the abyss, presently serves as a place of imprisonment for some demonic spirits (Luke 8:31; 2 Peter 2:4).

Following Christ's millennial kingdom, Satan will be released from the abyss and launch a final revolt against God: "When the thousand years are ended, Satan will be released from his prison and will come out to deceive the nations that are at the four corners of the earth, Gog and Magog, to gather them for battle; their number is like the sand of the sea" (Revelation 20:7-8).

Jerusalem will be the target city of this satanic revolt. This is significant, for Jerusalem will be the headquarters of Christ's government throughout the millennial kingdom (Isaiah 2:1-5). An attack against Jerusalem is ultimately an attack against Christ Himself.

The attack stands no chance of success. It is much like a canoe attacking a battleship. Scripture affirms that fire will instantly come down upon the invaders (Revelation 20:9).

Fire is a common mode of God's judgment against very serious offenses throughout biblical history: "The LORD rained on Sodom and Gomorrah sulfur and fire from the LORD out of heaven" (Genesis 19:24). Nadab and Abihu committed a very serious infraction, after which "fire came out from before the LORD and consumed them" (Leviticus 10:1-2). When people complained against the Lord, "the fire of the LORD burned among them and consumed some outlying parts of the camp" (Numbers 11:1). Any who try to harm God's two prophetic witnesses during the tribulation period will experience a fiery response: "If anyone would harm them, fire pours from their mouth and consumes their foes" (Revelation 11:5).

Following God's fiery destruction of the rebellious invaders, the devil will be "thrown into the lake of fire and sulfur" where the beast and the false prophet are, "and they will be tormented day and night forever and ever" (Revelation 20:10). Notice that all three persons of the satanic trinity—Satan, the antichrist, and the false prophet—will suffer the same dire destiny. The antichrist and the false prophet will be thrown into the lake of fire before the beginning of the millennial kingdom. They will have been burning there for 1,000 years when Satan will join them—and all three will continue to burn for all eternity. They will receive their just due.

The fallen angels (demons) who have long served under Satan will also be judged and cast into the lake of fire. Matthew 25:41 refers to "the eternal fire prepared for the devil and his angels." Hence, the demonic spirits who have been harassing human beings throughout the ages will one day receive a just judgment!

FAST FACTS ON IMPRISONED ANGELS

Some fallen angels are already confined, awaiting future judgment. Jude 6 affirms, "The angels who did not stay within their own position of authority, but left their proper dwelling, he has kept in eternal chains under gloomy darkness until the judgment of the great day." Moreover, "God did not spare angels when they sinned, but cast them into hell and committed them to chains of gloomy darkness to be kept until the judgment" (2 Peter 2:4). These fallen angels may be the "sons of God" who committed heinous sexual sin with human women in Genesis 6.

Other demonic spirits remain free to continue their attacks on humans, especially believers in Christ (Matthew 12:43; Mark 1:23, 26; 3:28-30; 5:2, 8; 7:25; 9:25; Luke 4:33; 8:29; 9:42; 11:24; John 13:2, 27).

FAST FACTS ON SATAN THE DECEIVER

Deception has always been at the very heart of Satan's activities. It was through a lie that Satan brought spiritual and physical death to humankind (Genesis 3:4, 13; 1 John 3:8, 10-15). John 8:44 tells us, "He was a murderer from the beginning, and does not stand in the truth, because there is no truth in him. When he lies, he speaks out of his own character, for he is a liar and the father of lies." When Satan engages in deception, he is *in character*.

"Satan disguises himself as an angel of light" (2 Corinthians 11:14), blinds the minds of unbelievers (2 Corinthians 4:4), seeks to outwit Christians (2 Corinthians 2:11), and promotes lies (Acts 5:3). Christians must beware!

FAST FACTS ON THE DEPTHS OF HUMAN SIN

The very fact that there will be a massive human rebellion (instigated by Satan) at the end of Christ's millennial kingdom—a kingdom with an *absolutely perfect living environment*—shows the deep-reaching effects of human sin. Jesus often spoke of sin in metaphors that illustrate the havoc sin can wreak. He described sin as blindness (Matthew 23: 16-26), sickness (Matthew 9:12), being enslaved in bondage (John 8:34), and living in darkness (John 8:12; 12:35-46). Jesus also taught that both inner thoughts and external acts render a person guilty (Matthew 5:28; Mark 7:21-23). At the end of the millennial kingdom, unbelievers will succumb to their sin nature without restraint.

FREQUENTLY ASKED QUESTIONS

Why will God allow Satan to be released from the abyss after the millennial kingdom?

God's purpose seems to be to prove once and for all that the heart of every human being is desperately wicked (Jeremiah 17:9). Even in the best of environments—Christ's millennial kingdom, where there will be incredible physical and spiritual blessings—the fallen human heart will still have a great propensity to sin, and easily succumb to Satan's temptations to evil (Revelation 20:8-9).

Who will join sides with Satan in this final revolt?

After the tribulation, only believers will be invited into Christ's millennial kingdom (Matthew 25:31-46). But these redeemed people—all of them still in their mortal bodies—will still give birth to babies and raise children, some of whom will not necessarily follow Jesus.

When Satan is released at the end of the millennium, he will succeed in leading many of these unbelieving children—as well as grandchildren, and great-grandchildren, and the like—to revolt against Christ. "Their number is like the sand of the sea" (Revelation 20:8). This revolt will represent Satan's "last stand."

This rebellion is connected to "Gog and Magog" in Revelation 20:8. Is this the same Gog-Magog battle mentioned in Ezekiel 38?

No. There are too many differences in the descriptions of these respective battles. For example, the Ezekiel invasion involves a coalition of localized nations—Russia and some Muslim countries—that invade Israel. The revolt at the end of the millennial kingdom will involve people from around the world (Revelation 20:8).

The Ezekiel invasion will occur relatively soon after Israel's rebirth as a nation and the ingathering of Jews from around the world (Ezekiel 36–37). The invasion mentioned in Revelation 20:7-10 will occur after Jesus has been reigning on earth for 1,000 years.

Following the Ezekiel invasion, the Jews will spend seven months burying the dead invaders (Ezekiel 36–37). The invaders who partici-pate in Satan's revolt will be incinerated by fire (Revelation 20:9).

Following the Ezekiel invasion, the Jews will burn the invaders' weapons for seven years (Ezekiel 36–37). If this took place after the millennial kingdom, this burning of weapons for seven years would stretch into the eternal state, which doesn't make sense.

In Revelation 20:8, John used the phrase "Gog and Magog" not because these invasions are one and the same. Rather, Gog and Magog is a shorthand metaphor for a "massive evil invasion." John was indi-cating that Satan and his human rebels will launch a Gog-and-Magog-*like* invasion against Christ and His people.

TODAY'S BIG IDEAS

- After the millennial kingdom, Satan will be released from the abyss to lead one final revolt against God and His people.
- Jerusalem will be the target city of the satanic revolt.
- Many of the unbelieving descendants of the original believers who entered the millennial kingdom will join Satan in the rebellion. That these descendants choose not to follow Christ within the perfect environment of the millennial kingdom shows the deep-reaching effects of human sin.
- This rebellion against God and His people will be squashed instantly as fire descends upon them.
- The devil will be cast into the lake of fire following the revolt.

TODAY'S TRANSFORMING TRUTHS

- The human heart is capable of great wickedness and rebellion. Even Christians retain a sin nature and can find themselves in rebellion against God (Romans 7:15-20). Here's a threefold strategy for keeping rebellion in check: (1) Begin each day by stockpiling your mind with God's Word with a predetermined attitude of obedience (Psalm 119); (2) stay plugged in to Jesus throughout the day (John 15:1-11); and (3) walk moment-by-moment in dependence upon the Holy Spirit (Galatians 5:16-25).
- There is wisdom in "taking the long look." We can take the long look by considering how our choice to obey God today will bring blessing tomorrow. We can also take the long look by considering how our choice to disobey God will rob us of that blessing and bring only discouragement.

Day 37

The Great White Throne Judgment and the Lake of Fire

The state of our existence between physical death and the future resurrection is appropriately called the intermediate state. It is an *in-between* state—that is, the state of our existence *in-between* the time our mortal bodies die and the time we receive resurrection bodies in the future.

The intermediate state is a *disembodied* state. While one's physical body is in the grave, one's spirit or soul is either in heaven with Christ or in a place of great suffering apart from Christ. One's destiny in the intermediate state depends wholly upon whether one has placed faith in Christ during one's earthly existence.

The intermediate state of the ungodly dead is described in 2 Peter 2:9: "The Lord knows how to...keep the unrighteous under punishment until the day of judgment." The word "keep" in this verse is in the present tense, indicating that the wicked (unbelievers) are held captive and punished continuously. Peter portrays them as condemned prisoners being closely guarded in a spiritual jail while awaiting future sentencing and final judgment.

Those who have rejected Christ face a terrible judgment that will lead to them being cast into the lake of fire. It is called the great white throne judgment (Revelation 20:11-15). Christ will be the divine Judge, and those who will be judged are the unsaved dead from all of time. This judgment will occur after the millennial kingdom, Christ's 1,000-year reign on planet Earth.

Those who participate in the great white throne judgment will be resurrected for the very purpose of facing the divine Judge, Jesus Christ. During His earthly ministry, Jesus soberly announced that "an hour is coming when all who are in the tombs will hear his voice and come out, those who have done good to the resurrection of life, and those who have done evil to the resurrection of judgment" (John 5:28-29).

The wicked who face Christ at this judgment will be judged based on their works (Revelation 20:12-13). It is critical to understand that they get to this judgment because they are *already unsaved*. This judgment will not separate believers from unbelievers, for all who experience it will have already chosen, during their lifetimes, to reject God. Once they are before the divine Judge, they are judged according to their works not only to justify their condemnation but to determine the degree to which each person should be punished throughout eternity.

When Christ opens the Book of Life, no name of anyone present at the great white throne judgment is in it. Their names do not appear in the Book of Life because they have rejected the source of life—Jesus Christ.

> The **lake of fire** will be the eternal abode of Satan, the antichrist, the false prophet, and unbelievers from throughout all of history (Revelation 19:20; 20:10-15). All residents will be tormented day and night forever and ever. It is eternal.

The lake of fire is another term for hell. While hell is a real place, it was not part of God's original creation, which He called "good" (Genesis 1). Hell was created later to accommodate the banishment of Satan and his fallen angels, who rebelled against God (Matthew 25:41). Human beings who reject Christ will join Satan and his fallen angels in this infernal place of suffering (Revelation 20:11-15).

FAST FACTS ON BIBLICAL TERMS RELATED TO HELL

The Old Testament term *sheol* can have different meanings in different contexts. Sometimes the word means "grave." Other times it refers to the place of departed people in contrast to the state of living people. Sheol is viewed as a place of horror (Psalm 30:9), weeping (Isaiah 38:3), and punishment (Job 24:19).

Hades is the New Testament counterpart to sheol from the Old Testament. During the intermediate state, the rich man endured great suffering in Hades (Luke 16:19-31). Hades, however, is a temporary abode and will one day be cast into the lake of fire (Revelation 20:14).

One of the more important New Testament words translated "hell" (in Greek) is *gehenna* (Matthew 10:28). The original root of this word referred to a public rubbish dump where garbage was perpetually burned. It became an appropriate and graphic metaphor for hell.

Other terms for hell include unquenchable fire (Mark 9:43), the fiery lake of burning sulfur (Revelation 19:20), eternal fire (Matthew 18:8), eternal punishment (Matthew 25:46), destruction (Matthew 7:13), everlasting destruction (2 Thessalonians 1:8-9), the place of weeping and gnashing of teeth (Matthew 13:42), and the second death (Revelation 20:14).

The horror of hell is inconceivable to the human mind.

FREQUENTLY ASKED QUESTIONS

What is the "fire" of hell?

Many interpreters believe it is a literal fire. This is believed to explain why there is unending weeping and gnashing of teeth (Matthew 13:42).

Other interpreters believe "fire" is a metaphorical way of expressing the great wrath of God. Scripture tells us: "The LORD your God is a consuming fire, a jealous God" (Deuteronomy 4:24); "God is a consuming fire" (Hebrews 12:29); "His wrath is poured out like fire" (Nahum 1:6); "Who can stand when he appears? For he is like a refiner's fire" (Malachi 3:2); God said, "My wrath will flare up and burn like fire because of the evil you have done—burn with no one to quench it" (Jeremiah 4:4 NIV).

A third point of view is that the term "fire," in contexts dealing with hell, refers to *both* literal fire *and* the great wrath of God. This third view seems to best capture the sheer horror of hell as portrayed in Scripture.

Will the wicked dead have a second chance?

No. Scripture represents the state of unbelievers after death as a fixed state, and there is no second chance (Luke 16:19-31; John 8:21, 24; 2 Peter 2:4, 9; Jude 6-7, 13). Once a person has passed through the doorway of death, there are no further opportunities to repent and turn to Christ for salvation (Matthew 7:22-23; 10:32-33; 25:41-46). Hebrews 9:27 affirms, "It is appointed for man to die once, and after that comes judgment." Woe to those who reject Christ in this life.

Where does Scripture affirm that degrees of punishment will be handed out at the great white throne judgment?

The **degrees of punishment** in the lake of fire will be commensurate with the degrees of sinfulness among human beings.

In Matthew 11:20-24, Jesus spoke of things being more tolerable for some than others on the day of judgment. In Luke 12:47-48, Jesus spoke of the possibility of receiving a light beating versus a severe beating. Jesus also spoke of certain people who will receive a greater condemnation than others (Luke 20:47). Moreover, in John 19:11, Jesus spoke of greater and lesser sins, and thus greater and lesser guilt (see also Matthew 10:15; 16:27; Revelation 20:12-13; 22:12).

> Just as **believers** differ in how they respond to God's law, and therefore, in their reward in heaven, so **unbelievers** differ in their response to God's law, and therefore, in their punishment in hell. Just as there are **degrees of reward in heaven**, so there are **degrees of punishment in hell**. Our Lord is perfectly just in all things.

Does God really send people to hell?

Scripture tells us that God is "not wishing that any should perish, but that all should reach repentance" (2 Peter 3:9). God specifically sent Jesus into the world to pay the penalty for our sins by dying on the cross (John 3:16-17). Unfortunately, not all people are willing to admit that they sin, and they will not trust in Christ for forgiveness. They don't accept the payment of Jesus' death for them. So, God allows them to experience the harsh results of their choice (Luke 16:19-31).

C.S. Lewis once said that in the end, there are two groups of people. One group of people says to God, "Thy will be done." These are those who have placed their faith in Jesus Christ and will live forever with God in heaven. The second group of people are those to whom God says, sadly, "Thy will be done!" These are those who have rejected Jesus Christ and will spend eternity apart from Him.[32]

TODAY'S BIG IDEAS

- The wicked dead are presently incarcerated in spirit prison, where they await the future great white throne judgment.
- The wicked dead will be resurrected just prior to the great white throne judgment.
- The wicked dead will face Christ at the great white throne judgment. They will not only be condemned, but will also be assigned various degrees of punishment.
- Following the great white throne judgment, the wicked dead will be immediately cast into the lake of fire, where they will suffer for eternity.

TODAY'S TRANSFORMING TRUTHS

- The names of the wicked dead will not be found in the Book of Life. Christians can rejoice that their names *are* found in the Book of Life. Jesus instructed His followers, "Rejoice that your names are written in heaven" (Luke 10:20). What an awesome thing to ponder!
- I hate the idea of people suffering eternally in the lake of fire. To me, it is a motivation to regularly engage in apologetics and evangelism among unbelievers with a view to rescuing *as many people as possible* from a future spent in the lake of fire (Mark 16:15; Romans 1:16; 1 Corinthians 1:17; 2 Timothy 4:5; 1 Peter 3:15).

Day 38

The New Heavens
and the New Earth

The present heavens and earth will one day be destroyed. Following this, God will create a new heavens and earth. It's all part of God's "plan of the ages." And it's all for you and me!

While we might think it's a shame that our present beautiful earth will be destroyed, we need to look at the bigger biblical picture. Think back to the scene in the garden of Eden. Adam and Eve sinned against God. Not only were they kicked out of Eden, a curse was also placed on the earth by God in judgment (Genesis 3:17-18). At that time, the universe was "subjected to futility" and is now in "bondage to decay" (Romans 8:20-21 CSB). *This earth is running down.*

Before the eternal state can begin, God must deal with this cursed earth and universe. A related defilement is that Satan has long carried out his evil schemes on earth (Ephesians 2:2). Therefore, the earth must also be purged of all stains resulting from his extended presence here.

In short, the old must be destroyed to establish the new. Earth, along with the first and second heavens—the earth's atmosphere (Job 35:5) and the stellar universe (Genesis 1:17; Deuteronomy 17:3)—must be destroyed as a preface to the eternal state.

Scripture often speaks of the passing of the old heavens and earth. Psalm 102:25-26 says of God the Creator: "Of old you [O God] laid the foundation of the earth, and the heavens are the work of your hands. They will perish, but you will remain; they will all wear out like a garment. You will change them like a robe, and they will pass away" (insert added for clarity).

In Isaiah 51:6, we likewise read, "Lift up your eyes to the heavens, and look at the earth beneath; for the heavens vanish like smoke, the earth will wear out like a garment...but my salvation will be forever." This reminds us of Jesus' words in Matthew 24:35, "Heaven and earth will pass away, but my words will not pass away."

Perhaps the most extended section of Scripture dealing with the passing of the old heavens and earth is 2 Peter 3:

> The heavens and earth that now exist are stored up for fire, being kept until the day of judgment and destruction of the ungodly...The heavens will pass away with a roar, and the heavenly bodies will be burned up and dissolved, and the earth and the works that are done on it will be exposed...The heavens will be set on fire and dissolved, and the heavenly bodies will melt as they burn! But according to his promise we are waiting for new heavens and a new earth in which righteousness dwells (verses 7, 10, 12-13).

After the universe is cleansed by fire, and God creates new heavens and a new earth, all vestiges of the curse and Satan's presence will be utterly and forever removed from all creation. This means that the eternal abode of the redeemed will be blessed beyond the ability of words to describe. It is wondrous to ponder the complete absence of decay, sickness, sorrow, tears, and death. All things will be made new, and how blessed it will be!

FAST FACTS ON AN EXPANDED HEAVEN

There is a distinction between the *present* heaven—where God now dwells and where believers go at the moment of death (2 Corinthians 5:8; Philippians 1:21-23)—and the *future* heaven, where believers will spend all eternity (2 Peter 3:13; Revelation 21:1). Scripture reveals that a grand and glorious renovation is coming. One expositor explained the renovation this way: "God will renovate the heavens and the earth, merging His heaven with a new universe for a perfect dwelling-place that will be our home forever. In other words, heaven, the realm where

God dwells, will expand to encompass the entire universe of creation, which will be fashioned into a perfect and glorious domain fit for the glory of heaven."[33]

This means you and I can look forward to living eternally in a magnificent kingdom where both heaven and earth unite in a glory that exceeds the imaginative capabilities of the finite human brain. Finally, the prophecy of Revelation 21:1, 5 will be fulfilled: "Then I saw a new heaven and a new earth, for the first heaven and the first earth had passed away...And he who was seated on the throne said, 'Behold, I am making all things new.'"

What all this means is that one day heaven and earth will no longer be separate realms, as they are now, but will be merged. Believers will thus continue to be in heaven even while they are on the new earth. The new earth will be utterly sinless and hence bathed and saturated in the light and splendor of God, unobscured by evil of any kind or tarnished by evildoers of any description.

FAST FACTS ON A RENEWED UNIVERSE

The new heavens and new earth will be this present universe—only it will be purified of all evil, sin, suffering, and death.

> The Greek word used to designate the newness of the cosmos is not *neos*, but *kainos*. *Neos* means "new in time" or "new in origin." But *kainos* means "new in nature" or "new in quality." Hence, the phrase "new heavens and a new earth" refers not to a cosmos that is totally other than the present cosmos. Rather, the new cosmos will stand in continuity with the present cosmos, but it will be utterly renewed and renovated.

We will live on the same earth, but it will be gloriously rejuvenated, with no weeds, thorns, or thistles. The creation will be transformed, perfected, and purged of everything evil.

This means that a resurrected people will live in a resurrected universe! Matthew 19:28 thus speaks of "the regeneration" (KJV). Acts 3:21 speaks of the "restoration of all things."

Everything will be new in the eternal state. Everything will be according to God's glorious nature. The new heavens and the new earth will be brought into blessed conformity with all that God is—in a state of fixed bliss and absolute perfection.

FREQUENTLY ASKED QUESTIONS

What are the three heavens mentioned in Scripture?

The Scriptures refer to three heavens:

➲ The **first heaven** is the earth's atmosphere (Job 35:5).

➲ The **second heaven** is the stellar universe (Genesis 1:17; Deuteronomy 17:3).

➲ The **third heaven** is the ineffable and glorious dwelling place of God in all His glory (2 Corinthians 12:2). This third heaven is elsewhere called the "highest heaven" (1 Kings 8:27; 2 Chronicles 2:6).

Out of the three heavens, which ones become new?

Scripture reveals that the only heavens that have been negatively affected by humankind's fall are the first and second heavens. The entire physical universe is running down and decaying, so it will be renewed. The third heaven—God's perfect and glorious dwelling place—remains untouched by human sin. It needs no renewal. The only change that will come is that heaven will be expanded to include the new heavens (earth's atmosphere and the stellar universe) and the new earth.

Why will there be no sea on the new earth?

About three-quarters of the earth's surface is presently covered with water and is therefore uninhabitable. By contrast, on the new earth, there will be no sea (Revelation 21:1). This means there will be an immensely increased land surface, making the whole world inhabitable. The life principle in this new earth will not be water, but rather, the water of life (22:1).

Bible expositors observe that for some people, the sea calls to mind the great destructive flood of Noah's time. For other people, the sea constitutes a barrier between loved ones, who may live on opposite sides of the ocean. Keep in mind that as the apostle John wrote the book of Revelation, he was exiled on the island of Patmos, surrounded by water on every side and thereby prevented from contact with his loved ones throughout Asia Minor (Revelation 1:9). There will be no sense of separation on the new earth. Fellowship will never be broken!

TODAY'S BIG IDEAS

- In preparation for the eternal state, God will first destroy the old heavens and the old earth.

- All vestiges of sin and Satan must be removed from the present creation.

- God will then create a new heavens and earth, which will be especially suited for the eternal state.

TODAY'S TRANSFORMING TRUTHS

- You and I have relatively short lifespans. To us, it can seem like the planets and stars have been around forever. But they haven't. They were created. Only God is eternal. *Two things are worthy of reflection:* (1) God is awesome and is truly worthy of our praise; and (2) God is deserving of our utmost thanks for the eternal life He gives us in Jesus Christ (John 3:16).

- Go outside on a clear night and look straight up. Are you impressed with the starry universe? Christ created it all (John 1:3; Colossians 1:16). He's a great Designer, *yes?* But you haven't seen anything yet. Christ will one day create new heavens and a new earth—as well as the eternal city called the New Jerusalem (Revelation 21). All of this is part and parcel of "what no eye has seen, nor ear heard, nor the heart of man imagined, what God has prepared for those who love him" (1 Corinthians 2:9). It will be incredible!

Day 39

The New Jerusalem
and the Eternal State

Jesus informed His followers that He would "prepare a place" for them in the Father's house in heaven (John 14:1-3). This "place" is the New Jerusalem.

The description of the New Jerusalem in Revelation 21:11-25 is astounding. Presented to our amazed gaze is a scene of such transcendent splendor that the human mind can scarcely take it in. This is a scene of ecstatic joy. The voice of the One identified as the Alpha and the Omega, the beginning and the end, utters a climactic declaration: "Behold, I am making all things new" (Revelation 21:5).

The words contained in Revelation 21 and 22 no doubt evidence the limited human terminology available to describe the utterly indescribable. The New Jerusalem will be a place of unimaginable splendor, greatness, excellence, and beauty. It will be far more wondrous than we can imagine.

It is particularly worth noting that the city is designed to reflect and manifest the incredible glory of God. We are told that "the city has no need of sun or moon to shine on it, for the glory of God gives it light, and its lamp is the Lamb" (Revelation 21:23). Scripture reveals that the city is transparent—strategically designed to transmit the glory of God in the form of light without hindrance. The human imagination is simply incapable of fathoming the immeasurably resplendent glory of God that will be perpetually manifest in the eternal city. This is especially so when one considers that all manner of precious stones will be built into the eternal city.

The New Jerusalem will rest upon the new earth. It will be a perfect environment in every way!

FAST FACTS ON THE NEW JERUSALEM

The New Jerusalem will be immense, measuring approximately 1,500 miles by 1,500 miles by 1,500 miles. The city will be tall enough, in today's terms, to reach about one-twentieth of the way to the moon from the earth's surface. If the city has stories that are 12 feet high, the city will have 600,000 stories.

Some believe the New Jerusalem will be shaped like a pyramid. This would explain how the river of the water of life could flow down its sides as pictured in Revelation 22:1-2. Others view it as shaped like a cube, much like the Holy of Holies in Solomon's Temple (1 Kings 6:20).

The city will have high walls and open gates (Revelation 21:12). The walls will have 12 foundations, and on each foundation will be written a name of one of the 12 apostles (Revelation 21:14). This will serve as an eternal reminder that the church was built upon these men of God (Ephesians 2:20).

There will be angels at each of the 12 gates, not only as guardians, but also to function as ministering spirits to the heirs of salvation (Hebrews 1:14). The names of the 12 tribes of Israel will be written on the gates, perhaps to remind us that "salvation is from the Jews" (John 4:22). The city's gates will never be shut, and there will be no night there (Revelation 21:25). There will never again be any external threat.

Major features of this eternal city include the river of life and the tree of life with its healing leaves (Revelation 22:1-2). It will be a holy city (Revelation 21:1-2). There will be no sin or unrighteousness of any kind here. As I've heard said with a touch of humor, "There will be no need for cops and lawyers."

FAST FACTS ON THE GRAND REVERSAL

God will bring about an incredible grand reversal for us. "In the beginning, God created the heavens and the earth" (Genesis 1:1). In the eternal state, new heavens and a new earth await us (Revelation 21:1-2). In the beginning, the sun and moon were created as "two great lights" (Genesis 1:16-17). The eternal state entails an eternal city where there is no longer any need for such light, for the glory of God lights up the eternal city of the redeemed (Revelation 21:23; 22:5).

In the beginning, God created the night (Genesis 1:5). The eternal state involves a nightless eternity (Revelation 22:5). In the beginning, God created the seas (Genesis 1:10). The new earth in the eternal state will no longer have a sea (Revelation 21:1).

In the beginning, human beings succumbed to Satan's temptations (Genesis 3:1-4). In the eternal state, Satan will be eternally quarantined from the people of God (Revelation 20:10). In the beginning, God pronounced a curse following humankind's fall into sin (Genesis 3:17). In the eternal state, there will be no more curse (Revelation 22:3).

In the beginning, paradise was lost (Genesis 3:23-24). In the eternal state, paradise will be gloriously restored for redeemed humans (Revelation 2:7). In the beginning, Adam and Eve were barred from the tree of life (Genesis 3:22-24). In the eternal state, redeemed humans will enjoy restoration to the tree of life (Revelation 2:7; 22:2, 14, 19). In the beginning, tears, death, and mourning entered human existence (Genesis 2:17; 29:11; 37:34). In the eternal state, tears, death, and mourning will be forever absent from the redeemed (Revelation 21:4).

How wondrous it will all be!

FREQUENTLY ASKED QUESTIONS

Is the river of the water of life
in the New Jerusalem a literal river?

In Revelation 22:1-2, John says, "Then the angel showed me the river of the water of life, bright as crystal, flowing from the throne of God and of the Lamb through the middle of the street of the city." Some take this river to be merely symbolic; others take it literally. The best approach is to take it *literally and symbolically*. It is a real river that symbolizes the rich abundance of the spiritual life of the redeemed in the eternal city. Just as a river provides a perpetual outflow of thirst-quenching water on a sunny day, perhaps the river of the water of life symbolizes the perpetual provision of spiritual satisfaction and blessing to the redeemed, who are now basking in the warm glow of eternal life.

In what way do the leaves on the tree of life provide for the "healing" of nations?

The Greek word for "healing" in Revelation 22:2 is *therapeia*, from which the English word *therapeutic* is derived. The word carries the basic meaning of "health-giving." In the present context, the word conveys the idea that the leaves on the tree of life perpetually give spiritual health to the redeemed peoples of the world. These leaves have nothing to do with correcting any ills, for such ills will not exist.

How will the New Jerusalem be different from earthly cities?

The New Jerusalem will be better than earthly cities in every way imaginable. For example, earthly cities constantly have to be rebuilt or repaired, but no such repair will ever be necessary in the New Jerusalem. Believers and unbelievers live in earthly cities, but only believers will be present in the eternal city.

Many people go hungry and thirsty in earthly cities, but no one will hunger or thirst in the New Jerusalem. Earthly cities have crime, but there will be perfect righteousness in the eternal city. Earthly cities often have outbreaks of rebellion, but there will be no such rebellion in the heavenly city. All will be in submission to the divine King, Jesus Christ.

People in earthly cities have many broken relationships, but all relationships in the New Jerusalem will be perfect and loving. Widespread disease is common in earthly cities, but perfect health will predominate in the New Jerusalem. Earthly cities have graveyards, but such will be absent in the eternal city. (Death will be entirely foreign to our experience in heaven.) Earthly cities get dark at night, but the eternal city will always be lighted.

Our existence in heaven will be entirely unlike our experience on earth. The eternal city, the New Jerusalem, is going to be incredible, far more so than any human mind could fathom or even begin to imagine. As 1 Corinthians 2:9 puts it, we will experience "what no eye has seen, nor ear heard, nor the heart of man imagined."

TODAY'S BIG IDEAS

- The eternal habitat for the saints of all ages will be an eternal city called the New Jerusalem.

- The New Jerusalem will be a place of unimaginable splendor, greatness, excellence, and beauty.

- This New Jerusalem will rest upon the new earth. Its central features include the river of life and the tree of life.

- God and humankind will dwell there for all eternity.

TODAY'S TRANSFORMING TRUTHS

- Life on earth is a mere dot in time. Life in heaven is an endlessly long line. Live for the line, not the dot (Matthew 6:19-21). As Charles Spurgeon put it, "Time is short. Eternity is long. It is only reasonable that this short life be lived in the light of eternity."[34]

- Matthew Henry said, "It ought to be the business of every day to prepare for our last day."[35] There is much wisdom here.

- Jonathan Edwards made several resolutions I've adopted as my own. Here are two of them: (1) "Resolved, that I will live so as I shall wish I had done when I come to die." (2) "Resolved, to endeavor to my utmost to act as I can think I should do, if I had already seen the happiness of heaven, and hell's torments."[36]

Day 40

Living in Light of Eternity

Each of us should live with a strong sense of expectancy as we ponder the wonder of heaven and the afterlife. Think about it:

- Believers who die before the rapture have their spirits depart from the body and go straight into the Lord's presence in heaven. Their spirits will then be reunited with resurrected bodies at the future rapture.

- Believers who are alive on earth at the time of the rapture will be instantly translated into their glorified bodies.

- From that moment forward, *believers will always be with Christ.*

These fabulous truths about our eternal future ought to have a life-changing impact on how we live in the present. The two big areas of life change, in my thinking, are (1) living righteously and (2) maintaining an eternal perspective.

I find it highly relevant that many prophetic Bible verses are immediately followed by an appeal to live in righteousness and personal purity. For example, the apostle Paul advised that because the day of salvation (the rapture) is drawing so very near, Christians ought to "walk properly" and avoid such things as getting drunk, sexual immorality, quarreling, and jealousy (Romans 13:11-14).

Peter likewise urged that because "the end of all things is at hand," we should "therefore be self-controlled and sober-minded" (1 Peter 4:7). We should also show love and hospitality (verses 8-9).

John speaks of Christ's future appearing in 1 John 3:2-3 and then urges, "Everyone who thus hopes in him purifies himself as he is pure."

The appearance of Christ that John speaks of pertains to the future rapture. Since the rapture could occur at any moment, let's live pure lives!

Bible prophecy can also motivate us to live with an eternal perspective. This kind of perspective involves keeping our eyes on heaven, staying aware of our mortality, and resolving to live in light of eternal realities.

One of my all-time favorite Bible passages is Colossians 3:1-2: "If then you have been raised with Christ, seek the things that are above, where Christ is, seated at the right hand of God. Set your minds on things that are above, not on things that are on earth." As great as Colossians 3:1-2 is in English, it is even richer—and far more intense— in the original Greek. It communicates the idea, "Diligently, actively, single-mindedly think on the realities of heaven." It is also a present tense in the Greek. This conveys continuous action. The verse communicates the idea, "Perpetually keep on thinking about the realities of heaven...Make it an ongoing process, 24/7."

FAST FACTS ON BEING WITH CHRIST IMMEDIATELY FOLLOWING DEATH

Following the moment of death, we will go directly into the presence of the Lord Jesus in heaven. At death, the spirit (or soul) slips out of the physical body just as easily as a hand slips out of a glove (see Genesis 35:18; 2 Corinthians 5:8; Philippians 1:21-23).

When this happens, the "clothing" of the body is no longer on the spirit, so we experience a sense of "nakedness" (2 Corinthians 5:1-4). But don't worry: This sense of nakedness is only temporary—we'll eventually receive new clothing: a resurrection body.

Ecclesiastes 12:7 affirms that at the moment of death, "The spirit will return to God who gave it." Right before Jesus died, He prayed to the heavenly Father, "Father, I entrust my spirit into your hands" (Luke 23:46 NLT). Before Stephen died, he prayed, "Lord Jesus, receive my spirit" (Acts 7:59).

Paul exulted, "My desire is to depart and be with Christ, for that is far better" (Philippians 1:23). Because the spirit departs the body and goes to be with the Lord at death, we need not fear death: "We are fully confident, and we would rather be away from these earthly bodies, for then we will be at home with the Lord" (2 Corinthians 5:8).

FAST FACTS ON THE IMMINENCE OF THE RAPTURE

The rapture could occur at any moment—it is imminent. Remember, the term *imminent* means "ready to take place" or "impending." The apostle Paul thus said that "time is running out" and "our salvation is nearer now than when we first believed" (Romans 13:11 NLT). He said this because the rapture is imminent.

Paul exulted that we "eagerly wait" for the Lord Jesus Christ (1 Corinthians 1:7; Philippians 3:20). He said, "The Lord is coming soon" (Philippians 4:5). Indeed, we "are looking forward to the coming of God's Son from heaven" (1 Thessalonians 1:10). We live in constant expectancy of the rapture.

The rapture is a *signless* event. There are no prophecies awaiting fulfillment before it occurs. This is in contrast to the second coming of Christ, which has seven years of prophetic signs preceding it during the tribulation period (Revelation 4–18).

FAST FACTS ON RESURRECTED BODIES

Prophetic Scripture affirms that our resurrection bodies will be just like the resurrection body of Jesus (Philippians 3:21; 1 John 3:2). Because Jesus' resurrection body was physical, so, too, will our resurrection bodies be physical.

Numerous scriptures affirm that Jesus' resurrection body was physical. It was missing from the tomb after the resurrection (Matthew 28; Mark 16; Luke 24; John 20), and even retained the crucifixion scars (Luke 24:39; John 20:27). The resurrected Jesus verbally affirmed He was not a spirit but rather had real flesh and bones (Luke 24:39). He also ate food in His resurrection body, thus proving His body was physical (Luke 24:30, 42-43; John 21:12-13). He was physically touched by others on a number of occasions (Matthew 28:9; John 20:27-28).

Like Jesus, you and I will be physically resurrected from the dead.

FREQUENTLY ASKED QUESTIONS

Will we have a reunion with our Christian loved ones in heaven?

Yes. In the Old Testament, when Ishmael was 137 years old, "he breathed his last and died, and was *gathered to his people*" (Genesis 25:17; emphasis added). When the text says he was gathered to his people, the meaning is that he joined other loved ones in the afterlife who were believers.

The same thing happened with Jacob. Genesis 49:33 tells us that "when Jacob finished commanding his sons, he drew up his feet into the bed and breathed his last and was *gathered to his people*" (emphasis added). Likewise, "Isaac breathed his last, and he died and was *gathered to his people*" (Genesis 35:29; emphasis added; see also Numbers 27:12-13; Judges 2:10).

At death, the believer's spirit departs the body and is reunited with other believing family members and friends in heaven. They are "gathered to" other believers in the afterlife.

Consider the Thessalonian Christians. They were very concerned about their Christian loved ones and friends who had died. They expressed their concern to the apostle Paul. In 1 Thessalonians 4:13-17, Paul assured the Thessalonians that there will indeed be a reunion in heaven. They should therefore comfort each other in this realization (verse 18).

Will we recognize each other in heaven?

Yes, I believe so. In 1 Thessalonians 4:13-17, Paul taught the Thessalonian Christians that they would be reunited with their Christian loved ones, and therefore they ought to comfort one another with this reality. There would be little comfort if we did not recognize each other in the afterlife.

When David's son died, he expressed confidence that he would be reunited with him in heaven. "Now he is dead...Can I bring him back again? I shall go to him, but he will not return to me." David would "go to him" in the afterlife. David's great anticipation of a reunion in the afterlife would make little sense if he were unable to recognize his son (2 Samuel 12:23).

Luke 16:19-31 is even more explicit. Jesus speaks about the rich man and Lazarus, who died and were in the afterlife. Abraham was also there. All three recognized each other.

In Luke 20:38, Jesus refers to the God "of the living" and indicates that Abraham, Isaac, and Jacob are living with God in the afterlife. This implies that Abraham, Isaac, and Jacob are still recognized as Abraham, Isaac, and Jacob in the afterlife.

Given this scriptural evidence, we can all rejoice that we will recognize our Christian loved ones in the afterlife.

TODAY'S BIG IDEAS

- We can live with a strong sense of expectancy because we will all receive incredible body upgrades.

- Bible prophecy serves as a strong motivation to live righteously and in purity.

- Bible prophecy is a strong incentive to live with an eternal perspective.

- It is wise to daily ponder the realities of heaven in a diligent, active, and single-minded way.

- Part of keeping an eternal perspective is having a constant awareness of our mortality. Earthly life is just a dot within eternity.

TODAY'S TRANSFORMING TRUTHS

- Have you lost a Christian loved one in death? Most of us have. And it still hurts. But our separation won't last long. A reunion is coming (1 Thessalonians 4:13-17). And once that reunion arrives, we'll never again be separated from our Christian loved ones. The apostle Paul therefore urges, "Encourage one another with these words" (verse 18).

- I've noticed that I've slowed down a lot. That's what aging has done to me. I can no longer leap up the stairs like I used to. I now feel occasional back pains when lifting heavy objects. Add into the mix a few joint pains here and there. The older I get, the more my body runs down. (*Can you relate?*) But my resurrected/glorified body will be eternally youthful, eternally vigorous, and eternally strong. God uses the aging process to cause us to yearn for the things of eternity—including our body upgrades.

A Closing Reflection:

Stockpiling Your Mind with God's Thoughts

Christians can rest assured of their destiny in heaven, where things will be wonderful forever. Meanwhile, there is no denying that hard times are ahead for all the inhabitants of this tiny planet. Christians will miss the worst of it because they will be raptured prior to the tribulation period. But even the events transpiring in the world today can be highly distressing.

After giving it considerable thought, I have chosen to close our 40-day tour through prophetic Scripture with a simple admonition:

> ➲ **Immerse yourself in the comforting truths of God's Word.**
>
> ➲ **Put another way: Stockpile your mind with God's thoughts.**

When I teach on the Bible, I always like to point out:

- The Bible is much like a *manufacturer's handbook* that instructs us how to operate our lives.
- The Bible is also like a pair of *glasses* for out-of-focus eyes. Without the glasses, we do not see clearly. We see only a blurred reality. But with the glasses, all comes into clear focus. We see things as they really are.
- The Bible is also like a *lamp*. It sheds light on our path and

helps us to see our way clearly. Psalm 119:105 says, "Your word is a lamp to my feet and a light for my path."

- The Bible is also like *food* (Hebrews 5:12; 1 Peter 2:2). It gives us spiritual nourishment. If we do not consistently feed on God's Word, we become spiritually malnourished.

- The Bible is also like a *love letter* or Valentine's card— from God to us (John 3:16-17). It tells us about how God's great love for us motivated Him to send Jesus into the world to die for our sins so we could be saved.

- Lastly, the Bible is like an *anchor*. Just as an anchor keeps a boat from floating away, so the Bible is an anchor for us. It prevents us from being swept away when a tidal wave of adversity comes our way.

During these end times, it is critically important for Christians to stay deeply rooted in God's Word. Below, I've listed some of my favorite verses as a starting point for you.

As you look up each of the verses, meditate on the truth you learn. The Hebrew word for *meditate* carries the idea of "murmuring." It pictures an individual reading and concentrating so intently on what he's reading in Scripture that his lips move as he reads. Such Christian meditation fills our minds with godly wisdom and insight. Scripture affirms, "Blessed is the man...[whose] delight is in the law of the LORD, and on his law he meditates day and night" (Psalm 1:1-2).

Continued meditation on these truths causes them to become a part of the fabric of our lives. I therefore urge you to take the time to feast your soul on the following verses. *Don't rush:*

MAINTAIN FAITH IN GOD:

Blessed are those who trust—Jeremiah 17:7.
Do not throw away trust—Hebrews 10:35.
Faith grows from hearing God's Word—Romans 10:17.
Faith is the certainty of what we do not see—Hebrews 11:1.
Live by faith, not sight—2 Corinthians 5:7.

Small faith yields big results—Luke 17:5-6.
Trust in the Lord with a whole heart—Proverbs 3:5.
Trust in the Lord, not man—Psalm 118:8.
Without faith, it is impossible to please God—Hebrews 11:6.

KEEP YOUR HOPE FIRM:

Maintain confident assurance—Hebrews 11:1.
Enjoy everlasting comfort and hope—2 Thessalonians 2:16-17.
God's plans involve hope—Jeremiah 29:11.
Hope in God—Psalms 39:7; 43:5; Lamentations 3:24.
Hope in God's unfailing love—Psalm 33:18, 20, 22.
Hope in God's Word—Romans 15:4.
Those who hope in the Lord renew their strength—Isaiah 40:31.

STAY OPTIMISTIC—NO MATTER WHAT:

Be confident—2 Corinthians 5:6-7.
Be joyful always—1 Thessalonians 5:16.
Be strong and take heart—Psalm 31:24.
Rejoice and be glad—Psalm 118:24.
Lift your eyes to the hills—Psalm 121:1.
Don't fear bad news—Psalm 112:7-8.

DO NOT WORRY:

God's antidote to worry—Philippians 4:6-7.
Cast your anxiety upon God—1 Peter 5:7.
Circumstances need not cause worry—Luke 8:22-25.
God consoles us—Psalm 94:19.
Jesus' advice on anxiety—Matthew 6:25-34.

BE FAITHFUL TO GOD—NO MATTER WHAT:

Be a faithful servant—Matthew 25:23.
Choose today whom you will serve—Joshua 24:15.
Be faithful in small matters—Luke 16:10.
The fruit of the Spirit includes faithfulness—Galatians 5:22.

God preserves the faithful—Psalm 31:23.
Keep a firm grip on everything taught to you—2 Thessalonians 2:15.
Cling to God's truth—Hebrews 4:14.
Listen carefully to the truths you've learned—Hebrews 2:1.
The Lord guards the faithful—Psalm 97:10.
Stand true to what you believe—1 Corinthians 16:13.
Stay true to the Lord—Philippians 1:27.
Remain faithful—2 Timothy 3:14.

Thomas Watson (1620–1686)—Puritan preacher and author—once said, "Leave not off reading the Bible till you find your hearts warmed...Let it not only *inform* you, but *inflame* you" (emphasis added).[37]

This is similar to something George Müller (1805–1898) once said. He affirmed that his first priority each morning was "to have my soul happy in the Lord...I saw that the most important thing I had to do was to give myself to the reading of the Word of God and to meditation on it."[38]

End-time Christians need to have hearts that are inflamed by the Word of God and souls that are happy in the Lord. We ought to make these our top priorities. We ought to be "Psalm 1 Christians"—that is, Christians who are blessed because their delight is in the Word of God (Psalm 1:2). This is the way to survive and thrive during these last days.

Make it so!

Bibliography

Ankerberg, John, and Dillon Burroughs. *Middle East Meltdown*. Eugene: Harvest House, 2007.

Feinberg, Charles. *The Prophecy of Ezekiel*. Eugene: Wipf and Stock, 2003.

Fruchtenbaum, Arnold. *The Footsteps of the Messiah*. San Antonio: Ariel, 2004.

Geisler, Norman. *Systematic Theology* vol. 4, *Church/Last Things*. St. Paul: Bethany House, 2005.

Hays, J. Daniel, J. Scott Duvall, and C. Marvin Pate. *Dictionary of Biblical Prophecy and End Times*. Grand Rapids: Zondervan, 2007.

Hitchcock, Mark. *Bible Prophecy*. Wheaton: Tyndale House, 1999.

———. *Iran: The Coming Crisis*. Sisters: Multnomah, 2006.

———. *Is America in Bible Prophecy?* Sisters: Multnomah, 2002.

———. *The Coming Islamic Invasion of Israel*. Sisters: Multnomah, 2002.

———. *The Late Great United States*. Colorado Springs: Multnomah, 2009.

———. *The Second Coming of Babylon*. Sisters: Multnomah, 2003.

Hoyt, Herman. *The End Times*. Chicago: Moody, 1969.

Ice, Thomas, and Randall Price. *Ready to Rebuild: The Imminent Plan to Rebuild the Last Days Temple*. Eugene: Harvest House, 1992.

Ice, Thomas, and Timothy Demy. *Prophecy Watch*. Eugene: Harvest House, 1998.

———. *What the Bible Says About Heaven and Eternity*. Grand Rapids: Kregel, 2000.

———. *When the Trumpet Sounds*. Eugene: Harvest House, 1995.

LaHaye, Tim. *The Beginning of the End*. Wheaton: Tyndale, 1991.

———. *The Coming Peace in the Middle East*. Grand Rapids: Zondervan, 1984.

LaHaye, Tim, and Jerry Jenkins. *Are We Living in the End Times?* Carol Stream: Tyndale, 1999.

LaHaye, Tim, and Thomas Ice. *Charting the End Times*. Eugene: Harvest House, 2001.

Pentecost, J. Dwight. *Things to Come*. Grand Rapids: Zondervan, 1964.

Price, Randall. *Fast Facts on the Middle East Conflict*. Eugene: Harvest House, 2003.

———. *Unholy War*. Eugene: Harvest House, 2001.

Prophecy Study Bible, ed. Tim LaHaye. Chattanooga: AMG Publishers, 2001.

Rhodes, Ron. *40 Days through Daniel*. Eugene: Harvest House, 2016.

———. *40 Days through Revelation*. Eugene: Harvest House, 2013.

———. *Basic Bible Prophecy*. Eugene: Harvest House, 2021.

———. *Bible Prophecy Answer Book*. Eugene: Harvest House, 2017.

———. *End-Times Super Trends*. Eugene: Harvest House, 2017.

———. *Israel on High Alert*. Eugene: Harvest House, 2018.

———. *Jesus and the End Times*. Eugene: Harvest House, 2019.

———. *New Babylon Rising*. Eugene: Harvest House, 2019.

———. *Northern Storm Rising: Russia, Iran, and the Emerging End-Times Military Coalition Against Israel*. Eugene: Harvest House, 2008.

———. *The 8 Great Debates of Bible Prophecy*. Eugene: Harvest House, 2014.

———. *The End Times in Chronological Order*. Eugene: Harvest House, 2012.

————. *The Middle East Conflict: What You Need to Know.* Eugene: Harvest House, 2009.

————. *The Popular Dictionary of Bible Prophecy.* Eugene: Harvest House, 2010.

————. *The Topical Guide of Bible Prophecy.* Eugene: Harvest House, 2010.

————. *Unmasking the Antichrist.* Eugene: Harvest House, 2012.

————. *What Happens After Life?* Eugene: Harvest House, 2014.

Rosenberg, Joel. *Epicenter: Why Current Rumblings in the Middle East Will Change Your Future.* Carol Stream: Tyndale, 2006.

Ruthven, Jon Mark. *The Prophecy that Is Shaping History: New Research on Ezekiel's Vision of the End.* Fairfax: Xulon, 2003.

Showers, Renald. *Maranatha: Our Lord Come!* Bellmawr: The Friends of Israel Gospel Ministry, 1995.

The Popular Bible Prophecy Commentary, eds. Tim LaHaye and Ed Hindson. Eugene: Harvest House, 2006.

The Popular Encyclopedia of Bible Prophecy, eds. Tim LaHaye and Ed Hindson. Eugene: Harvest House, 2004.

Walvoord, John F. *End Times.* Nashville: Word, 1998.

————. *Jesus Christ Our Lord.* Chicago: Moody, 1980.

————. *The Millennial Kingdom.* Grand Rapids: Zondervan, 1975.

————. *The Prophecy Knowledge Handbook.* Wheaton: Victor, 1990.

————. *The Return of the Lord.* Grand Rapids: Zondervan, 1979.

Walvoord, John F., and Mark Hitchcock. *Armageddon, Oil, and Terror.* Carol Stream: Tyndale House, 2007.

Yamauchi, Edwin. *Foes from the Northern Frontier: Invading Hordes from the Russian Steppes.* Eugene: Wipf and Stock, 1982.

Scripture Copyright Notifications

Notes

1. I recommend Steve Miller, *Foreshadows: 12 Megaclues That Jesus' Return Is Nearer Than Ever* (Eugene: Harvest Prophecy, 2022).

2. Mark Hitchcock, *The Amazing Claims of Bible Prophecy* (Eugene: Harvest House, 2010), Kindle.

3. Tim LaHaye and Ed Hindson, *The Essential Guide to Bible Prophecy* (Eugene: Harvest House, 2012), Kindle.

4. Mark Hitchcock, *Seven Signs of the End Times* (Sisters: Multnomah, 2009), Kindle.

5. J.C. Ryle, *Heaven* (Rosshire, Great Britain: Christian Focus Publications, 2000), 40.

6. David Cooper, cited in Arnold Fruchtenbaum, *The Footsteps of the Messiah* (San Antonio: Ariel Ministries, 1983), n.p., insert added in place of the less understood word "axiomatic."

7. Thomas Constable, "Dr. Constable's Expository Notes," in The Bible Study App, Olive Tree Bible Software, 2021.

8. Charles Ryrie, *The Basis of the Premillennial Faith* (Dubuque: ECS Ministries, 2005), n.p.

9. Dwight L. Moody, comp. Emma Moody Fitt, *The D.L. Moody Year Book* (New York: Revell, 1900), 80.

10. George Barna, *America at the Crossroads* (Grand Rapids: Baker Books, 2016), 41.

11. David Kinnaman and Gabe Lyons, *Good Faith: Being a Christian When Society Thinks You're Irrelevant and Extreme* (Grand Rapids: Baker Books, 2016), 12-13.

12. Barna, *America at the Crossroads,* 51.

13. Barna, *America at the Crossroads,* 33, 67.

14. Paul Feinberg, "2 Thessalonians 2 and the Rapture," *When the Trumpet Sounds,* eds. Thomas Ice and Timothy Demy (Eugene: Harvest House, 1995), 308.

15. William MacDonald and Arthur L. Farstad, *Believer's Bible Commentary* (Nashville: Thomas Nelson, 2016), in the Bible Study App, Olive Tree Bible Software, 2022.

16. Albert Barnes, *Notes on the New Testament*, vol. 8, *2 Corinthians* (Grand Rapids: Baker, 1996), 105.

17. Charles C. Ryrie, *Basic Theology* (Chicago: Moody, 1999), 581.

18. Tim LaHaye and Jerry Jenkins, *Are We Living in the End Times?* (Wheaton: Tyndale House, 1999), 281.

19. Walter K. Price, *The Coming Antichrist* (Neptune: Loizeaux Brothers, 1985), 145.

20. Price, *The Coming Antichrist,* 146-47.

21. Mark Hitchcock, *The Complete Book of Bible Prophecy* (Wheaton: Tyndale House, 1999), 199-200.

22. Thomas Constable, "Notes on Revelation," Available online at www.soniclight.com/constable/notes/pdf/revelation.pdf.

23. Renald Showers, *Maranatha: Our Lord Come!* (Bellmawr: The Friends of Israel Gospel Ministry, 1995), 43.

24. Ed Hindson, "False Prophet," in *The Popular Encyclopedia of Bible Prophecy*, eds. Tim LaHaye and Ed Hindson (Eugene: Harvest House, 2004), 103.

25. David Reagan, "The Rise and Fall of the Antichrist," *RaptureReady*, at https://www.raptureready.com/2014/09/07/the-rise-and-fall-of-the-antichrist-by-dr-david-r-reagan/.

26. John F. Walvoord, "Revelation," in *The Bible Knowledge Commentary: New Testament*, eds. John F. Walvoord and Roy B. Zuck (Wheaton: Victor Books, 1983).

27. Henry C. Thiessen, cited in Renald Showers, *Maranatha: Our Lord Come!* (Bellmawr: Friends of Israel, 1995), 50.

28. David Jeremiah, *The Coming Economic Armageddon: What Bible Prophecy Warns About the New Global Economy* (New York: FaithWords, 2010), 146.

29. John F. Walvoord, *The Final Drama: Fourteen Keys to Understanding the Prophetic Scriptures* (Grand Rapids: Kregel, 1997), 125.

30. Thomas Ice and Timothy Demy, *The Coming Cashless Society* (Eugene: Harvest House, 1996), 132.

31. Thomas Ice, "God's Purpose for Israel During the Tribulation," *Pre-Trib Research Center*, at https://www.pre-trib.org/articles/all-articles/message/god-s-purpose-for-israel-during-the-tribulation/read.

32. C.S. Lewis, *The Great Divorce* (San Francisco: HarperOne, 2009), 26.

33. John MacArthur, *The Glory of Heaven* (Wheaton: Crossway, 1996), 90.

34. Ron Rhodes, *1001 Unforgettable Quotes About God, Faith, and the Bible* (Eugene: Harvest House, 2011), Kindle.

35. Rhodes, *1001 Unforgettable Quotes*, Kindle.

36. Rhodes, *1001 Unforgettable Quotes*, Kindle.

37. Rhodes, *1001 Unforgettable Quotes*, Kindle.

38. Rhodes, *1001 Unforgettable Quotes*, Kindle.

Other Great Harvest House Books by Ron Rhodes

Basic Bible Prophecy
40 Days Through Genesis
40 Days Through Daniel
40 Days Through Revelation
The Big Book of Bible Answers
Commonly Misunderstood Bible Verses
Find It Fast in the Bible
The Popular Dictionary of Bible Prophecy
Understanding the Bible from A to Z
The 8 Great Debates of Bible Prophecy
Cyber Meltdown
New Babylon Rising
End Times Super Trends
Jesus and the End Times
The End Times in Chronological Order
Northern Storm Rising
Unmasking the Antichrist
Spiritual Warfare in the End Times
Israel on High Alert
The Secret Life of Angels
What Happens After Life?
Why Do Bad Things Happen If God Is Good?
The Wonder of Heaven
Reasoning from the Scriptures with the Jehovah's Witnesses
Reasoning from the Scriptures with the Mormons
The Coming Oil Storm (eBook only)
The Topical Handbook of Bible Prophecy (eBook only)

To learn more about our Harvest Prophecy resources, please visit:

www.HarvestProphecyHQ.com

HARVEST PROPHECY
An Imprint of Harvest House Publishers